McGraw-Hill/Contemporary's

Language Builder

Introductory

Mc Graw Hill Wright Group

Series Editor: Rebecca Grazulis
Executive Editor: Linda Kwil
Marketing Manager: Sean Klunder
Production Manager: Genevieve Kelley
Cover Designer: Michael E. Kelly

 **Wright Group**

ISBN 0-07-283586-9

Send all inquiries to:
Wright Group/McGraw-Hill
One Prudential Plaza
130 East Randolph Street, Suite 400
Chicago, IL 60601

Printed in the United States of America.

8 9 10 CUS 13 12 11

◆ Contents

Contents *continued*

To the Learner

If you have had problems expressing your ideas, particularly in writing, Contemporary's *Language Builder* will help. The workbook will explain basic grammar and composition skills and let you practice those skills in focused exercises. *Language Builder* will increase your confidence in your ability to communicate, both orally and in writing.

How does using Contemporary's *Language Builder* improve your language skills, particularly writing skills? The workbook covers these areas:

- grammar and usage
- sentence formation
- paragraph development
- capitalization
- punctuation
- writing conventions for special forms, like letters and quotations

Included in the workbook are a Pretest and a Posttest. The Pretest will help you find your language strengths and weaknesses. Then you can use the workbook lessons to improve your skills. When you have finished the lessons and exercises, the Posttest will help you see if you have mastered those skills. Usually mastery means answering 80 percent of the questions correctly.

Language Builder will help you develop specific language skills, especially writing skills. Each workbook is self-contained with the Answer Key at the back of the book. Clear directions will guide you through the lessons and exercises.

Each lesson in the workbook is divided into four parts.

 Introduce clearly defines, explains, and illustrates the skill. The examples prepare you for the work in the following exercises.

 Practice lets you work on the skill just introduced. If a skill requires additional explanation, this page (and, rarely, **Apply**) may add to the information presented in **Introduce.**

C **Apply** gives you a different way to practice the skill.

 Check Up provides a quick test on the skill covered in the lesson.

How to Use This Workbook

1. Take the Pretest on pages 7–14. Check your answers with the Answer Key on page 15. Refer to the Evaluation Chart to find which skills you need to work on.

2. Take each four-page lesson one at a time. Ask your teacher for help with any problems you have.

3. Use the Answer Key, which begins on page 199, to correct your answers after each exercise.

4. At the end of each unit, read the Unit Review and complete the Unit Assessment. These pages provide an opportunity to combine all the individual skills you have worked on and to check your progress on them. After the Unit Assessment, your teacher may want to discuss your answers with you.

5. After you have finished all six units, take the Posttest on pages 190–197. Check your answers on page 198. Then discuss your progress with your teacher.

◆ Pretest

Decide which punctuation mark, if any, is needed in each sentence.

1. No I have never been to Europe.

   A ,

   B ?

   C "

   D None

2. "Don't forget to lock the door,"
   Nathan said.

   F ,

   G ?

   H "

   J None

3. Hit the brakes

   A ?

   B !

   C ,

   D None

4. Abby whispered, The movie is
   about to start."

   F "

   G ,

   H ?

   J None

Choose the word or phrase that best completes each sentence.

5. This is the _____ day of the
   year.

   F hotter

   G more hot

   H hottest

   J most hottest

6. The plane _____ on the runway.

   A has landing

   B is land

   C has landed

   D land

7. A new band _____ at the club
   last night.

   F will play

   G was play

   H were played

   J played

8. City workers _____ the trash
   every Friday.

   A was collecting

   B collect

   C has collected

   D collects

Choose the sentence that is written properly and shows the correct capitalization and punctuation. Be sure the sentence you choose is complete.

9. F Touching the ball after the whistle.

    G The player with the most points.

    H Is a season ticket holder.

    J The coach spoke to reporters.

10. A the hikers went down into the canyon.

    B leave the package by the door.

    C "when can we see the new house?" asked Grace.

    D When the bell rings, the fight stops.

11. F Let's go home it's getting late.

    G The moon is full tonight.

    H Snow is falling the roads are icy.

    J Turn right I live in the gray house.

12. A The Scotts go to Canada every July.

    B Lila always uses coupons at the grocery Store.

    C Do you know the letters in the greek alphabet?

    D Pam graduated from mercer High School.

13. F The principal themself welcomed us.

    G Send your report to I by the end of the day.

    H The head chef himself made dessert.

    J The boss asked for them names an hour ago.

14. A I heard this joke before but I forgot them.

    B Celeste put her bank card into the machine.

    C The nurse which I spoke to earlier is off duty now.

    D Ted made themselves an iced tea.

15. F It's not polite to stare.

    G I just know wer'e going to be late.

    H Your'e the third person to ask me that question.

    J My dog isnt' used to big crowds.

16. A I couldn't never lie to you.

    B It won't do no good to cry.

    C Aren't there any cupcakes left?

    D Phil couldn't hardly remember his lines in the play.

Read the two underlined sentences. Then choose the sentence that <u>best</u> combines those sentences.

17. <u>Blake drives a minivan.</u>
    <u>The minivan is red.</u>

    F When Blake drives a minivan, it is red.

    G A red minivan is the kind of car that Blake drives.

    H When Blake drives, his minivan is red.

    J Blake drives a red minivan.

18. <u>Janette works for the city.</u>
    <u>Luis works for the city.</u>

    A Janette and Luis work for the city.

    B When Janette works for the city, so does Luis.

    C Either Janette or Luis works for the city.

    D If Luis works for the city, Janette does, too.

19. <u>Kevin barbecues ribs in his backyard.</u>
    <u>Kevin barbecues ribs often.</u>

    F Ribs are often barbecued in Kevin's backyard.

    G Kevin's ribs are often are barbecued in his backyard.

    H Kevin often barbecues ribs in his backyard.

    J When ribs are barbecued, Kevin often barbecues them in his backyard.

20. <u>Clare answered the phone.</u>
    <u>Clare took a message.</u>

    A Clare took a message as she answered the phone.

    B When Clare took the message, she answered a phone.

    C Clare answered the phone and took a message.

    D A phone was answered by Clare, who took the message.

Read each paragraph. Then choose the sentence that best fills the blank.

21. _____. Little kids dig in the sand. Older children swim and play volleyball. Parents relax on a blanket. And everyone enjoys a picnic supper at the beach.

    F A trip to the beach is fun for the whole family.

    G Parents must watch their children closely at the beach.

    H It is hard to find trips that the whole family likes.

    J Older children often choose not to come on family outings.

22. _____. E-mail reaches the recipient in an instant. Regular mail may take between two and four days. E-mail often seems cold. A handwritten note, on the other hand, seems warm and friendly.

    A E-mail and regular mail are alike in many ways.

    B E-mail and regular mail are quite different.

    C Only people who have time to spare use regular mail these days.

    D Send your messages by e-mail whenever you can.

23. Anita worked hard on Carla's birthday cake. First she baked the cake. _____. Next she frosted the cake. Finally, she put three candles on it.

    F Then she chose Carla's favorite kind of cake.

    G Then she made the frosting.

    H Then she lit the candles.

    J Then she cut Carla a slice of the cake.

24. Roy and Maria clean the garage together. _____. Then they sweep the empty garage floor. They hose the floor down and move everything back in. The job is done for another year.

    A They move everything out of the garage.

    B The garage gets pretty dirty during the year.

    C They take a short work break.

    D They drive their cars back into the garage.

Read each topic sentence. Then choose the answer that best develops the topic sentence.

25. Lila and Charles check for two things before they stay in any motel room.

    F Many motels are part of a chain. Motels in a chain are similar in quality.

    G Motels by the side of the freeway usually meet their standards. Rooms can be rented most weeknights.

    H They demand that the room not smell like stale smoke. They also want good beds.

    J The word *motel* combines *motor* and *hotel*. Motels first appeared after cars were invented.

26. Athletes who like extreme sports are a breed apart.

    A Extreme sports are popular today. One extreme sport is hang gliding.

    B Some extreme sports are not legal. Climbing the outside of buildings is one example.

    C New equipment has made these sports possible. Athletes trust better materials.

    D A normal, safe sport will not keep these athletes happy. They need anger and challenge.

27. The northern lights make a great sky show.

    F Another name for the northern lights is aurora borealis. There are also southern lights.

    G They flicker across the sky for thousands of miles. The lights are often green but can also be red and purple.

    H Northern lights are natural. They happen when bits of energy from the sun are trapped around the earth.

    J Most people will never see the northern lights. This display can be seen only near the North Pole.

Read each paragraph. Then choose the sentence that does <u>not</u> belong in the paragraph.

28.   **1.** Ida Lewis saved many lives. **2.** Ida was the keeper of the Lime Rock Lighthouse. **3.** She rescued at least 18 people from drowning. **4.** Keeping a lighthouse was a lonely job.

A Sentence 1

B Sentence 2

C Sentence 3

D Sentence 4

29.   **1.** Breakfast is an important meal. **2.** A good breakfast gives you energy to start the day. **3.** Blueberry pancakes are a popular breakfast. **4.** People who do not eat a hearty breakfast are more likely to eat junk food before lunch.

F Sentence 1

G Sentence 2

H Sentence 3

J Sentence 4

30.   **1.** The local food bank helps people in need. **2.** Many cities have people who cannot afford to buy food. **3.** At the food bank, volunteers fill bags with different kinds of food. **4.** Needy families can pick up these bags of groceries for free.

A Sentence 1

B Sentence 2

C Sentence 3

D Sentence 4

31.   **1.** Jim goes to sleep every night at ten o'clock. **2.** Much activity goes on in your brain when you sleep. **3.** Every night, you have four to six sleep cycles. **4.** You dream at least once during each cycle.

F Sentence 1

G Sentence 2

H Sentence 3

J Sentence 4

Read the letter and the paragraphs, and look at the underlined parts. Choose the answer that is written correctly for each underlined part.

(32)   <u>may 20, 2003</u>

Sawtooth Dude Ranch
(33) <u>1357 pine street</u>
(34) <u>Boise, Idaho, 83705</u>

(35) <u>Dear Sir or Madam:</u>

(36) <u>Im'</u> planning a trip to Idaho this summer. A friend of mine stayed at your ranch last year. She said she had a wonderful time there. Please send me information about your daily and weekly rates.

(37)   <u>Sincerely yours</u>

Rose Fazio

Rose Fazio

32. A May, 20, 2003
    B may 20 2003
    C May 20, 2003
    D Correct as is

33. F 1357 pine street
    G 1357 Pine Street
    H 1357 Pine street
    J Correct as is

34. A Boise, Idaho 83705
    B Boise Idaho 83705
    C Boise Idaho, 83705
    D Correct as is

35. F Dear Sir or Madam,
    G Dear sir or madam,
    H Dear Sir Or Madam
    J Correct as is

36. A I'm
    B I'm'
    C Im
    D Correct as is

37. F sincerely, yours,
    G Sincerely yours,
    H Sincerely Yours,
    J Correct as is

(38) On November 2, people in <u>mexico celebrate</u> a holiday called the Day of the Dead. On that day, they remember family

(39) members <u>which</u> have died. People eat bread and candies in the

(40) shape of skulls. They <u>happily</u> march in parades with fake coffins. This part of the day is fun. But later people may visit the cemetery.

(41) There they <u>lights</u> candles and pray for the spirits of those who have passed away.

38. A Mexico Celebrate
 B Mexico celebrate
 C Mexico. Celebrate
 D Correct as is

40. A happier
 B more happier
 C happy
 D Correct as is

39. F whose
 G that
 H who
 J Correct as is

41. F light
 G is lighted
 H is lighting
 J Correct as is

(42) The sun can be your <u>skins</u> worst enemy. Its rays can cause

(43) problems from sunburn to <u>skin cancer, for</u> that reason, you should

(44) take steps to protect yourself from the <u>sun. try</u> to stay indoors

(45) from 10 A.M. to 3 P.M. <u>Wear sunscreen. When you</u> are outdoors. Respect the power of the sun.

42. A skins's
 B skins'
 C skin's
 D Correct as is

44. A sun. Try
 B sun, Try
 C sun, try
 D Correct as is

43. F skin cancer for
 G skin cancer. For
 H skin cancer for,
 J Correct as is

45. F Wear sunscreen. when you
 G Wear sunscreen, When you
 H Wear sunscreen when you
 J Correct as is

Pretest Answer Key and Evaluation Chart

This Evaluation Chart will help you find the language skills you need to study. Circle the questions you answered incorrectly and go to the practice pages covering those skills.

Key

1.	A	28.	D
2.	J	29.	H
3.	B	30.	B
4.	F	31.	F
5.	H	32.	C
6.	C	33.	G
7.	J	34.	A
8.	B	35.	J
9.	J	36.	A
10.	D	37.	G
11.	G	38.	B
12.	A	39.	H
13.	H	40.	D
14.	B	41.	F
15.	F	42.	C
16.	C	43.	G
17.	J	44.	A
18.	A	45.	H
19.	H		
20.	C		
21.	F		
22.	B		
23.	G		
24.	A		
25.	H		
26.	D		
27.	G		

Tested Skills	Question Numbers	Practice Pages
pronouns	13	23–26, 27–30
antecedent agreement	14, 39	31–34
verbs	6, 7	35–38, 39–42, 43–46
subject/verb agreement	8, 41	47–50
adjectives and adverbs	5, 40	51–54, 55–58, 59–62
use of negatives	16	63–66
sentence recognition	9, 11, 43, 45	71–74, 75–78
sentence combining	17, 18, 19, 20	79–82, 83–86, 87–90, 91–94
topic sentences	21, 22	99–102, 103–106
supporting sentences	25, 26, 27	107–110, 111–114
sequence	23, 24	115–118, 119–122
unrelated sentences	28, 29, 30, 31	123–126
proper nouns and proper adjectives	12, 38	131–134, 135–138
first words	10, 44	139–142
end marks	3	147–150
commas	1	151–154, 155–158, 159–162
quotations	2, 4	167–170, 171–174
apostrophes in contractions and possessives	15, 36, 42	175–178, 179–182
letter parts	32, 33, 34 35, 37	183–186

Correlation Chart

Correlations Between Contemporary's Instructional Materials and TABE™ Language

Language   Pretest Score _____   Posttest Score _____

Subskill	TABE™ Form 7	TABE™ Form 8	Practice and Instruction Pages			
			Language Builder Introductory	Pre-GED Language Arts, Writing	Complete Pre-GED	English Exercises (1–5)*
27 Usage						
pronouns	9, 36	9, 37, 44	23–26, 27–30	30–40	46–47, 78–82	1: 19–21
antecedent agreement	18, 42	40	31–34	41–44	82	1: 22 3: 9
verb tenses	8, 11, 45, 49, 53	5, 6, 12, 34, 39, 55	35–38, 39–42, 43–46	51–66	48–49, 89–111	1: 12–18 3: 5–6
subject/verb agreement	6, 15	7, 49	47–50	67–76	113–124	2: 8–18
adjectives and adverbs	7, 43, 48	50, 52	51–54, 55–58, 59–62	81–94	49–51, 127–132	1: 23–25, 27–28
use of negatives	37, 54	18	63–66	91–92		1: 26
28 Sentence Formation						
sentence recognition	12, 23, 38, 46	10, 13, 38, 54	71–74, 75–78	13–18	57–68	2: 3–7, 23–26 4: 9–10
sentence combining	24, 25, 26 27	20, 21, 22, 23 24, 25	79–82, 83–86 87–90, 91–94	101–110	139–148	2: 19–22
29 Paragraph Development						
topic sentences	30, 31	28, 29	99–102 103–106	157–161	150–155	3: 15–16
supporting sentences	32, 33	30, 31	107–110, 111–114		150–155	3: 27–28
sequence	28, 29	26, 27	115–118, 119–122	165–169	150–155	3: 22
unrelated sentences	34, 35	32, 33	123–126	165–169	150–155	3: 17–18

* Numbers correspond to the following titles: 1 = *Mastering Parts of Speech*; 2 = *Using Correct Sentence Structure*; 3 = *Improving Writing Style and Paragraphing*; 4 = *Building Punctuation Skills*; 5 = *Improving Spelling and Capitalization*

Subskill	TABE™ Form 7	TABE™ Form 8	Practice and Instruction Pages			
			Language Builder Introductory	*Pre-GED Language Arts, Writing*	*Complete Pre-GED*	*English Exercises (1–5)**
30 Capitalization						
proper nouns and proper adjectives	14, 17, 19, 22, 55	11, 14, 19, 35	131–134, 135–138	23–24, 133–138	71–74	5: 18–20, 23
first words	10	17, 45	139–142	134	59	5: 17, 22, 25
31 Punctuation						
end marks	1, 3, 13	1, 8, 36, 46	147–150	19–21, 139–140	59	4: 3–4
commas	5, 16, 20, 47, 50	3, 16, 48, 53	151–154, 155–158, 159–162	141–144	142–143, 149, 166–169	4: 5–8, 11
32 Writing Conventions						
quotations	2, 4, 21, 51	2, 4	167–170, 171–174	145–146	133–134	4: 22–25
apostrophes	52	15, 51	175–178, 179–182	27–28, 146, 149–150	83	4: 17–19
letter parts	39, 40, 41, 44	41, 42, 43, 47	183–186		105–107	5: 24

Corresponds to TABE™ Forms 7 and 8
Tests of Adult Basic Education are published by CTB Macmillan/McGraw-Hill.
Such company has neither endorsed nor authorized this test preparation book.

Nouns

Each word in our language has a special use.
Words with the same use are grouped and called a
part of speech. A **noun** is a part of speech that names
a person, place, or thing.

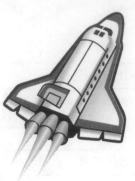

> The <u>shuttle</u> took <u>astronauts</u> into <u>space</u>.

Nouns can be common or proper. A **common noun**
is the general name of any person, place, or thing.

> The <u>mules</u> carried heavy <u>bags</u>.

A **proper noun** is the name of a particular person, place,
or thing. Every word in a proper noun begins with a
capital letter.

> <u>Marcia</u> hiked into the <u>Grand Canyon</u>.

A **singular** noun names one person, place, or thing.
A **plural** noun names more than one.

> The <u>ranger</u> (singular noun) pointed out rare <u>flowers</u>
> (plural noun).

Underline the nouns in each sentence.

1. Put the newspaper inside the front door.

2. Jack plays football in college.

3. It was hard to see the Golden Gate Bridge in the fog.

4. The pilot will land the plane in Detroit.

5. Austin is the capital of Texas.

6. These paintings by Georgia O'Keeffe show huge flowers.

7. Listen for birdcalls in the forest.

8. George Washington was known for his honesty.

9. In April tulips bloom in the garden.

10. Some members of the team were late for the game.

B ▶ Practice

On the line beside each noun, write *S* for singular or *P* for plural.

1. signs _____
2. boxes _____
3. judge _____
4. babies _____
5. house _____

6. fly _____
7. children _____
8. moon _____
9. lunches _____
10. women _____

Read each sentence. Does it have proper nouns that need to be capitalized? If so, rewrite them correctly on the line. If the proper nouns are capitalized properly, write *Correct* on the line.

11. Children dress up in costumes for halloween.

    _____

12. When did Lincoln write the Gettysburg Address?

    _____

13. Many tourists visit the eiffel tower in paris, france.

    _____

14. Will the new york yankees win the world series?

    _____

15. The ship sank in the atlantic ocean.

    _____

C Apply

On the line beside each common noun, write a matching proper noun. For example, a proper noun to match the common noun *river* might be *Ohio River*.

1. person   _____

2. school   _____

3. team   _____

4. state   _____

5. country   _____

Write a noun on each line to complete these sentences. Make sure it fits the description in parentheses ( ).

6. This bus stops at _____ (proper) and at Cherry Street.

7. Put cherries and _____ (plural) in the bowl.

8. Which _____ (singular) will you wear to the game?

9. The bug I fear the most is the _____ (common).

10. The fans clapped when a band called _____ (proper) stepped onstage.

11. Many people say that _____ (proper) is a great city.

12. Lee served a _____ (singular) to her guest.

13. The _____ (plural) made too much noise this morning.

14. We like to see the _____ (common) at the zoo.

15. In bad weather, _____ (plural) should not leave the harbor.

Circle the letter of the phrase that describes the underlined word in each sentence.

1. No animal runs faster than the <u>cheetah</u>.

   A common noun

   B proper noun

   C plural noun

   D None of these

2. The hounds chased the <u>fox</u> into a hollow log.

   F common noun

   G proper noun

   H plural noun

   J None of these

3. Will <u>elephants</u> still be around in 100 years?

   A proper noun

   B singular noun

   C plural noun

   D None of these

4. Marc is saving for a trip to <u>Africa</u>.

   F proper noun

   G plural noun

   H common noun

   J None of these

5. The lazy <u>dog</u> slept most of the day.

   A plural noun

   B proper noun

   C common noun

   D None of these

6. <u>Bats</u> are the only mammals that can fly.

   F singular noun

   G proper noun

   H plural noun

   J None of these

7. My birthday is in <u>January</u>.

   A common noun

   B proper noun

   C plural noun

   D None of these

8. The cab driver put our bags <u>in</u> the trunk.

   F plural noun

   G singular noun

   H common noun

   J None of these

A Introduce

Personal Pronouns

Pronouns are words used in place of nouns. One kind of pronoun is a **personal pronoun**. Personal pronouns often refer to people and are used in place of their names.

> Sara overslept, so <u>she</u> was late. (*She* refers to *Sara*.)

Personal pronouns can also refer to things.

> Sara set the alarm for 7:00. <u>It</u> didn't go off this morning. (*It* refers to *alarm*.)

Personal pronouns can be grouped within three categories:

Number: Pronouns can be singular or plural. If a noun is plural, the pronoun that replaces it must also be plural. Likewise, singular pronouns replace singular nouns.

Gender: Masculine pronouns refer to males (*he, him, his*). Feminine pronouns refer to females (*she, her, hers*). Neuter pronouns refer to neither gender (*it, its*).

Person: Speakers use **first person pronouns** to tell about themselves. When speakers are addressing someone else, they use **second person pronouns**. Speakers use **third person pronouns** to talk about other persons or things.

	Singular	Plural
First Person:	I, me, my, mine	we, us, our, ours
Second Person:	you, your, yours	you, your, yours
Third Person:	he, she, him, her, it, his, hers, its	they, them, their, theirs

Underline the personal pronoun in each sentence. Circle the word it refers to.

1. Iris waved to her friends.

2. The old tree spread its branches wide.

3. Ken ran fast, but he could not win the race.

4. Evie, Bill will pick you up at five o'clock.

5. Sharese knew the tune, but she couldn't recall the words.

6. Butterflies go through three stages before they become adults.

7. Brad, which of these coats is yours?

8. Jean said, "I need to make a phone call."

B Practice

Nominative pronouns are used as subjects in sentences.

I   we   you   he, she, it   they

We ride the bus every day.

He waited at the stop.

Objective pronouns are used as objects in sentences. Objects are commonly found after verbs or after prepositions, such as *to*, *for*, and *with*.

me   us   you   him, her, it   them

The driver saw me at the stop. (following the verb *saw*)

The bus stopped for her. (following *for*)

Underline the pronoun that completes each sentence correctly.

1. (We, Us) weeded the garden together.

2. The judges gave (he, him) first prize.

3. (She, Her) always orders vanilla ice cream.

4. The pitcher quickly threw the ball to (she, her).

5. (I, Me) will buy tickets for all the children.

6. (He, Him) can tell when rain is on the way.

7. The doctor gave (she, her) lotion for her dry skin.

8. (They, Them) played football in the snow.

9. The usher seated (we, us) in the last row.

10. I saw (they, them) at the market this morning.

11. I trained my dog to bring the stick back to (I, me).

12. (We, Us) were here first, so we should be seated before them.

13. (She, Her) learned how to sew a quilt from her mother.

14. Give your forms to (I, me) before you leave.

15. A loud noise awoke (he, him) in the middle of the night.

Apply

Some personal pronouns are called **possessive pronouns.**
Possessive pronouns show ownership.

> Helen dropped <u>her</u> fare in the box. (*Her* refers to *Helen*.)

The following is a list of possessive pronouns:

First Person:	my, mine	our, ours
Second Person:	your, yours	your, yours
Third Person:	his, her, hers, its	their, theirs

Some possessive pronouns have two forms. One form is used with a noun
(*my* name; *our* names; *your, her, its, their* name). The other form is used by itself
(*mine, ours, yours, hers, theirs*). Notice that possessive pronouns do not have
apostrophes.

> Gina, I have <u>your</u> coat. This coat is <u>yours</u>, isn't it?
> (*Your* is used with *coat*. *Yours* is used alone.)

Pronouns must match the words they refer to in gender, number, and person.

> Leon lost <u>his</u> notebook. (Both *Leon* and *his* are singular,
> masculine, and third person.)

**Underline the possessive pronoun. Circle the word it refers to.
(Sometimes it may refer to another pronoun.)**

1. The spider slowly made its way across the field.

2. I know that the prize will be mine someday.

3. Mr. Jackson was surprised to hear a knock on his door.

4. The fans cheered for their favorite players.

5. The actor worried about forgetting his lines.

Underline the possessive pronoun that correctly completes each sentence.

6. Is this (you, your) key ring?

7. Put (my, mine) pills on the nightstand, please.

8. Which one of those cars is (her, hers)?

9. The swimmers left (theirs, their) towels by the pool.

10. Emily got (her, hers) hair cut in a new way.

Each sentence has one word underlined. Choose the answer that should be substituted for each underlined word.

1. Alice wants a CD for <u>his</u> birthday.
   - A her
   - B she
   - C theirs
   - D Correct as it is

2. <u>They</u> are all going to the movies.
   - F them
   - G their
   - H theirs
   - J Correct as it is

3. Please return the book to <u>we</u>.
   - A I
   - B us
   - C our
   - D Correct as it is

4. <u>Me</u> put too much salt on my eggs.
   - F I
   - G My
   - H Her
   - J Correct as it is

5. They say the extra point should be <u>their</u>, but I think they are wrong.
   - A there
   - B theirs
   - C them
   - D Correct as it is

6. When Dad was young, <u>him</u> had a paper route.
   - F his
   - G them
   - H he
   - J Correct as it is

7. Do you remember <u>my</u> name?
   - A mine
   - B me
   - C you
   - D Correct as it is

8. The staff sent <u>he</u> a get-well card.
   - F his
   - G him
   - H I
   - J Correct as it is

9. Are you going to <u>your</u> class reunion this year?
   - A you're
   - B yours
   - C you
   - D Correct as it is

A ◆ Introduce

More Pronouns

There are other types of pronouns besides personal and possessive. **Relative pronouns** relate one part of a sentence to another part. Examples of relative pronouns are *who, whom, whose, which,* and *that. Who, whom, whose* and *that* refer to people. *Which* and *that* refer to things.

> Rebecca is the actress <u>who</u> is in the play.

> The ice cream, <u>which</u> we bought today, will be our dessert.

The most common problem is choosing between *who* and *whom.* Use *who* in front of a verb. Use *whom* after a preposition, such as *to, for,* and *with.*

> Jack is the agent <u>who</u> will be helping you. (before verb *will be helping*)

> The man to <u>whom</u> you are speaking is my father. (after *to*)

Underline the pronoun that completes each sentence correctly.

1. The child (who, whom) is standing by the fence is my cousin.

2. (Who, Whose) tickets are these?

3. Bill spoke with a writer (who, whom) comes from South Africa.

4. The book (whom, that) I read yesterday is lost.

5. The child for (who, whom) the party was given is crying.

6. Amy called Rosa (who, which) is her best friend.

7. To (who, whom) did the customer speak?

8. The ice cream flavor (that, who) sells best is vanilla.

9. (Who, Whom) invented the game of basketball?

10. The statue, (which, whom) comes from China, is very old.

11. My uncle, (who, which) lives in New York, is a comedian.

12. The train (who, that) just left is going to Bismarck.

13. (Whom, Whose) football is lying in the grass?

Another type of pronoun is a **reflexive pronoun.** A reflexive pronoun reflects an action back onto a noun or pronoun used earlier in the sentence. The reflexive pronouns are *myself, ourselves, yourself, yourselves, himself, herself, itself,* and *themselves.*

> Kim treated <u>herself</u> to a banana split. (*Herself* refers to *Kim.*)

A reflexive pronoun must always refer to another word in the same sentence.

> Mitch and <u>myself</u> went to the museum. (incorrect)
> I wrote that note <u>myself</u>. (correct; *myself* refers to *I*)

Never use *hisself* or *theirselves.*

Underline the reflexive pronoun in each sentence. Circle the word it refers to.

1. Barb wants to do the whole job herself.

2. They took themselves too seriously.

3. The queen herself cut the ribbon.

4. Why don't you make yourself at home?

5. The children themselves planned the picnic.

6. I found myself fascinated by the movie.

7. Are you allowed to vote for yourself?

8. The dog bit itself on the hind leg.

9. The artist himself signed the painting.

10. We should give ourselves a round of applause.

Underline the reflexive pronoun that completes each sentence correctly.

11. My boss gave (himself, hisself) a raise.

12. Lori found (myself, herself) a new apartment.

13. The drivers (themselves, theirselves) avoided an accident.

14. I reminded (himself, myself) to wash the dishes.

C Apply

**Underline the relative or reflexive pronoun in each sentence.
Circle the word it refers to.**

1. This factory, which makes vans, was built ten years ago.

2. The baker who made the sweet rolls gave one to Jeff.

3. The door that leads to the basement is closed.

4. Emily gave herself first aid after the accident.

5. The crew saw themselves on television.

6. The owner himself locked the door every night.

7. I woke myself up from the bad dream.

8. The runner who crosses the finish line first gets the prize.

9. The waiter to whom we spoke earned a large tip.

10. You should remind yourself to lock the door.

**Complete this paragraph. Write a pronoun from the box that makes sense in
each blank.**

themselves		they
who	himself	which

  The people _____ boarded the Titanic were ready for a smooth

trip. The captain _____ was quite sure he would have a good

cruise. But then the ship hit an iceberg. The ship, _____ was

believed to be unsinkable, began to sink. People headed for the lifeboats, but

_____ couldn't find enough boats for everyone. Many of the people

were not able to save _____. About 1,500 lives were lost.

D ▸ Check Up

Identify the pronoun in each sentence.

1. The clown with the red hair squirted himself in the face.

    A clown

    B squirted

    C himself

    D face

2. The boys who are going to the movie left early.

    F who

    G going

    H boys

    J early

3. The dog itself brought these worn-out slippers.

    A itself

    B brought

    C slippers

    D dog

4. Paula just chewed my last stick of gum.

    F stick

    G my

    H of

    J Paula

5. The prince himself will choose a wife at the ball.

    A prince

    B himself

    C choose

    D wife

6. Any customer who has a ticket can enter the theater now.

    F has

    G enter

    H ticket

    J who

7. Helen planted the roses herself.

    A Helen

    B the

    C planted

    D herself

8. The fans could not see who caught the ball.

    F fans

    G who

    H see

    J ball

Antecedent Agreement

Pronouns are words used in place of nouns. The word the pronoun replaces is called its **antecedent**.

> The baby takes <u>her</u> nap from 2:00 to 3:30 each day.

> (The antecedent of the pronoun *her* is *baby*.)

Pronouns must agree with, or match, their antecedents in three ways. First, they must agree in **number**. If the antecedent is singular, the pronoun must be singular. If the antecedent is plural, the pronoun must be plural.

> The king sent <u>his</u> knights into battle. (singular, *king*)

> Lee wrapped the gifts and tied bows on <u>them</u>. (plural, *gifts*)

Second, pronouns must match their antecedents in **gender**. Pronouns and antecedents may be masculine (*he, him, his*), feminine (*she, her, hers*), or neuter (*it, its*).

> The coach blew <u>his</u> whistle. (masculine, *coach*)

> The queen spoke to <u>her</u> people. (feminine, *queen*)

> The oak tree lost <u>its</u> leaves. (neuter, *tree*)

Underline each pronoun. Circle its antecedent.

1. The soldiers saluted their captain.

2. Inez found her keys behind the dresser.

3. Brenda visits Uncle Bob to cheer him up.

4. Gina heard a poem and soon had it memorized.

5. Grandpa played pro ball when he was younger.

6. The knights fought for their king.

7. Nancy bought a magazine and read it in bed.

8. The fighters relaxed when they heard the bell.

9. The angry driver honked her horn at the cab.

10. The artist wrote his name at the bottom of the painting.

B ▶ Practice

In addition to agreeing in number and gender, pronouns must agree with their antecedents in **person**. You use **first person** when you talk about yourself. You use **second person** when you talk to someone else. You use **third person** when you talk about other persons or things.

> I blame <u>myself</u> for the accident. (first person, *I*)
>
> You can hear the bird singing in <u>your</u> tree. (second person, *You*)
>
> The owner signed the check for <u>his</u> employee. (third person, *owner*)

Like other pronouns, relative pronouns must agree with their antecedents. Use *who* and *whom* when the antecedents are people. Use *which* and *that* when the antecedents are not people.

> My aunt, <u>who</u> sat with us at the wedding, took us home.
>
> The table, <u>which</u> was made of glass, was cracked.

Circle the letter of the sentence in which the pronoun agrees with its antecedent.

1. **A** If you see my brother, tell her to call home.

   B If you see my brother, tell him to call home.

2. **A** Olive ordered a pizza and shared them with us.

   B Olive ordered a pizza and shared it with us.

3. **A** I'll make a cup of strong coffee for myself.

   B I'll make a cup of strong coffee for herself.

4. **A** The trees that I planted are doing well.

   B The trees whom I planted are doing well.

Underline the pronoun that agrees with its antecedent. Circle the antecedent.

5. John broke (his, her) leg skiing.

6. Liza failed the test because (you, she) didn't have 20/20 vision.

7. These matches won't light because (they, it) got wet.

8. The toddler (who, which) was wearing a pink dress fell down.

9. The prince chose the young woman to be (her, his) bride.

10. After hours of walking, we found that (you, we) were really tired.

Read each sentence. If it has a pronoun that does not agree with its antecedent, rewrite the sentence correctly on the line. If the sentence has no pronoun-antecedent errors, write *Correct* on the line.

1. The train that I usually take is not running today.

_____

2. When I peel an onion, your eyes water.

_____

3. The girls left their scarves on the bench.

_____

4. The judges looked at the dog carefully and gave them first prize.

_____

5. The author themselves came to the party.

_____

6. My daughter fell off her bike, but he got right back on.

_____

7. Our pilot, which had flown many hours, brought us down safely.

_____

8. Michelle told himself to do her best.

_____

9. Pull these weeds because I hate seeing it in the garden.

_____

10. We were happy when we saw the waiter coming to our table.

_____

D Check Up

Each sentence has a pronoun missing. Choose the pronoun that completes the sentence. Make sure the pronoun agrees with its antecedent.

1. Bob dropped _____ token in the cash box.

   A his

   B her

   C their

   D its

2. We _____ have never been to the Grand Canyon.

   F themselves

   G ourselves

   H itself

   J herself

3. The driver, _____ was late for a meeting, ran the red light.

   A whose

   B whom

   C who

   D which

4. Before you turn, put _____ turn signal on.

   F my

   G her

   H their

   J your

5. When I received the letters, I answered _____ quickly.

   A it

   B us

   C them

   D me

6. Remind Carol to take _____ umbrella.

   F his

   G her

   H its

   J their

7. The movie, _____ was shot in Aspen, will open next week.

   A which

   B who

   C what

   D whom

8. I waved to my sisters, and _____ saved me a seat.

   F it

   G he

   H she

   J they

Verbs

A **verb** is a word that names an action or a state of being. Every sentence has at least one verb. An **action verb** shows an action that the subject does.

> Flowers <u>grow</u> in the window box.

Verbs that show state of being are linking verbs. A **linking verb** links a noun with another noun or pronoun, or with an adjective that describes the noun. Common linking verbs include: *is, am, are, was,* and *were*.

> Pansies <u>are</u> Alice's favorite flowers.
>
> (*Are* links *Pansies* and *flowers*.)
>
> A pansy <u>is</u> colorful. (*Is* links *pansy* and *colorful*.)

Some verbs are used as **helping verbs** with other verbs. *Can, must, will, shall, were, have, should,* and *must* are some common helping verbs.

> Everyone <u>can see</u> the flowers from the street.
>
> Flowers <u>were sold</u> at the market.

Underline every verb and every helping verb. Write each linking verb on the lines provided.

1. Dale paid $8.00 for each ticket. _____

2. The store carries fans, but they have sold every one. _____

3. Hakeem is a painter. _____

4. Workmen for the driveway project have arrived. _____

5. When Grandfather came to this country, he was a child. _____

6. Someone should sew a name tag into each item of clothing.

   _____

7. The children must finish their work before they can play. _____

8. Why are bubbles round? _____

B Practice

Every verb has important forms called **principal parts**. The following chart names the three principal parts and gives examples of some verbs.

Present Tense	Past Tense	Past Participle
look	looked	(has) looked
use	used	(has) used
see	saw	(has) seen
find	found	(has) found

A **regular verb** is one whose past tense and past participle are both formed by adding *-ed* or *-d* to the present tense form. *Look* and *use*, for example, are regular verbs. An **irregular verb** is one whose principal parts do not follow this pattern. *See* and *find* are irregular verbs.

Examine the verbs in the following chart. Then in the fourth column write *R* after each of the regular verbs and *I* after each of the irregular verbs.

Present Tense	Past Tense	Past Participle	
act	acted	(has) acted	
bring	brought	(was) brought	
drive	drove	(has) driven	
jump	jumped	(has) jumped	
keep	kept	(has) kept	
ride	rode	(has) ridden	
run	ran	(has) run	
turn	turned	(has) turned	

Apply

Examine the following chart.

Present Tense	Past Tense	Past Participle
annoy	annoyed	(has) annoyed
blow	blew	(has) blown
elect	elected	(has) elected
has, have	had	(has) had
need	needed	(has) needed
paint	painted	(has) painted
prepare	prepared	(has) prepared
see	saw	(has) seen
sew	sewed	(has) sown
store	stored	(has) stored
study	studied	(has) studied
take	took	(has) taken
throw	threw	(has) thrown
train	trained	(has) trained

Using the chart above, underline the verb that makes sense for each sentence.

1. Who (sew, sewed) this beautiful quilt?

2. She (paint, painted) the bedroom a pale yellow.

3. The people (elected, have elected) John Adams, our second president, in 1797.

4. Strong winds (blew, has blown) leaves off the trees last night.

5. Talkers in the audience (annoyed, has annoyed) the piano player.

6. She (take, has taken) harsh steps.

7. Coach Anderson (train, trained) her squad every day this week.

8. The delivery boy (throw, has thrown) the newspaper into the rose bushes again!

9. Everyone but Les (seen, has seen) a shooting star.

10. The boys (prepare, prepared) a surprise for you.

D Check Up

Circle the letter of the verb that best completes each sentence.

1. Years ago, children _____ with hoops.

   A playing

   B played

   C has playing

   D were played

2. At the restaurant, seven kinds of pancakes _____.

   F serve

   G are serving

   H are served

   J served

3. This van _____ up to nine passengers.

   A can carry

   B are carry

   C has carry

   D is carried

4. The dancers' masks _____ by art students.

   F make

   G made

   H have maded

   J were made

Read the sentences below. Circle the letter of the sentence that is written correctly and makes the most sense.

5. A Ella waited for the express bus at the stop.

   B Ella was waited for the express bus at the stop.

   C The stop was waited by Ella for the express bus.

   D The stop has waited by Ella for the express bus.

6. F Steven do the dishes last night.

   G Steven did the dishes last night.

   H Steven was done the dishes last night.

   J Steven was done by the dishes last night.

7. A The tennis court has been a popular place.

   B The tennis court has a popular place.

   C The tennis court has be a popular place.

   D The tennis court been a popular place.

8. F The guests at the party were brought by different dishes.

   G Different dishes brought the guests at the party.

   H The guests at the party bringed different dishes.

   J The guests at the party brought different dishes.

Verbs and Their Tenses

A verb changes form to show the time of the action it describes. These different forms are the **tenses** of the verb. The present, past, and future tenses are the **simple tenses**.

> The rose <u>looks</u> pretty. The roses <u>look</u> pretty. (present)
>
> They <u>looked</u> even nicer yesterday. (past)
>
> They <u>will look</u> dry and wilted in a few days. (future)

The **present tense** indicates an action that happens now or on a regular basis, such as "The sun rises every day." Most present tense verbs follow the pattern shown below for *look*. *Has* and *be* are important exceptions.

> **look**: I look, you look, she looks, we look, they look
>
> **has**: I have, you have, he has, we have, they have
>
> **be**: I am, you are, it is, we are, they are

The **past tense** indicates an action that occurred in the past. It is the second principal part of a verb. The past tense of regular verbs are formed by adding *-ed* or *–d* to the present form. If you don't know the past tense of an irregular verb, check a dictionary.

The **future tense** indicates an action that has not yet happened but will occur in the future. It is formed by using a helping verb such as *will* or *shall* with the present form.

Underline every verb. Identify the tense of each verb by writing *Present*, *Past*, or *Future* on the line.

1. We ate chicken dinners three nights in a row. _____

2. The poet will speak at Holmes Library on Thursday. _____

3. Almost everyone remembers a favorite teacher. _____

4. The news program will start in 15 minutes. _____

5. Years ago, workers earned less than today. _____

6. People at the meeting received name tags. _____

7. I understand your question. _____

8. Ed fixed the engine easily. _____

B Practice

To choose the correct tense of a verb, pay attention to clues in the sentence. A **present tense** verb is used in a sentence with the action happening now.

> I <u>know</u> what you <u>mean</u>.
>
> (Action takes place right now.)

A **past tense** verb is used when the sentence shows action that has already happened.

> Bill <u>ran</u> down the road yesterday.
>
> (Action took place yesterday.)

A **future tense** verb is used when the sentence shows action that will happen in the future.

> We <u>will see</u> the baby tomorrow.
>
> (Action will happen tomorrow.)

Circle the letter of the verb that correctly completes the sentence.

1. We _____ snow tomorrow morning.
   - A shoveled
   - B will shovel
   - C were shoveling
   - D shovel

2. Every day my dog Kayla _____ for me at the door.
   - F waited
   - G waits
   - H is waited
   - J will waited

3. If you _____ in the sun too long you will get burned.
   - A lies
   - B will lying
   - C lay
   - D lie

4. Brian _____ the flowers whenever he saw that they were wilted.
   - F water
   - G watered
   - H will water
   - J were watered

5. Mom _____ her garden early tomorrow.
   - A weeded
   - B will weed
   - C weeds
   - D be weeding

C ▸ Apply

Complete each sentence with the present, past, or future form of the verb in parentheses. (In some sentences, more than one tense is correct.)

1. (fall) While we were sleeping, rain _____.

2. (enjoy) Next month the family _____ a raft trip.

3. (search) Jack _____ for his lost tools all day yesterday.

4. (play) Linda sings, and Alexi _____ guitar.

5. (listen) _____ to the weather forecast at 4 p.m.

6. (repair) Tomorrow the crew _____ the roof.

7. (hurry) Abigail _____ to the manager's office to

    pick up her check.

8. (chop) Ed _____ the vegetables for dinner.

9. (get) Yang _____ a haircut next weekend.

10. (end) This offer _____ at midnight tonight.

11. (sit) Marcy _____ next to the window.

12. (shop) Lalo _____ for groceries every Saturday morning.

13. (buy) Pam _____ pork chops at the butcher

    store yesterday.

14. (skate) Next week Riley _____ over to his

    grandma's house.

Circle the letter of the verb that best completes each sentence.

1. Last Sunday my son _____ the game.

   A watched

   B was watched

   C will watch

   D watches

2. Before the party last week, gardeners _____ bushes for several days.

   F pruned

   G prune

   H will prune

   J are pruning

3. I _____ to work late this morning.

   A come

   B will come

   C came

   D comed

4. Prices at this restaurant _____ recently.

   F will be rising

   G will rise

   H rise

   J rose

Read the sentences below. Pay special attention to verbs and their tenses. Circle the letter of the sentence that is written correctly.

5. A Everyone at the show was laugh at the skits.

   B Andy was played a clumsy dancer.

   C At the end of the show, all the actors took a bow together.

6. F A large cruise ship employs hundreds of workers.

   G As passengers come aboard, someone was taking their pictures.

   H Every day the cooks will preparing tasty meals.

7. A Fall classes started next week.

   B Students are sign up by mail and in person.

   C Mr. French will teach an accounting class.

8. F Last month, Mrs. Lacy invite eleven children to her son's birthday party.

   G While the children played games, Mrs. Lacy frosted a cake.

   H Timmy Lacy will thanked the guests for their gifts.

A ▸ Introduce

Perfect Tenses of Verbs

A **perfect tense** usually indicates action that is completed by a certain time. Each perfect tense verb combines a simple tense form of *have* with the past participle of the main verb. (The simple tense forms of *have* are these: present—*has, have*; past—*had*; future—*will have*.)

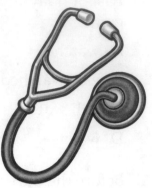

The **present perfect tense** indicates action that began in the past and continues in the present.

> Roger <u>has worked</u> as a doctor <u>for five years</u>.

The **past perfect tense** indicates action that was completed before another action in the past.

> He <u>had worked</u> in a hospital <u>before he went to medical school</u>.

The **future perfect tense** indicates action that will be completed before an action in the future.

> <u>By next June</u>, he <u>will have worked</u> for a total of ten years.

At least one verb in each item is in a perfect tense. Underline every verb. Then write each perfect tense verb on the line.

1. The college named its new building after Mr. Lewis. He had served on the

   board for many years. _____

2. Although Gail and Sarah have been coworkers for years, they met for the

   first time yesterday. _____

3. Ramon has a ticket for tomorrow's game. By tomorrow night, he will have

   seen every game in the series. _____

4. Michelle has written a romance novel and wants to find a publisher.

   _____

5. The three children who had wandered away from the camp this morning

   were found an hour ago. _____

6. Zubin sails whenever he has time. By the end of this cruise, he will have

   spent over ten months at sea. _____

B ▶ Practice

Read each pair of sentences. Circle the letter of the sentence that uses verb tenses correctly.

1. **A** You will sing in the choir before last week's performance.

   B You had sung in the choir before last week's performance.

2. **A** We have sung that song many times.

   B We sung that song many times.

3. **A** By next December, we sang "The Star-Spangled Banner" a thousand times.

   B By next December, we will have sung "The Star-Spangled Banner" a thousand times.

4. **A** Kevin had returned by the time you left.

   B Kevin will have returned by the time you left.

5. **A** I have checked my watch several times in the last hour.

   B I will check my watch several times in the last hour.

6. **A** Heather have walked a mile before we found her.

   B Heather had walked a mile before we found her.

7. **A** Your teacher has answered that question often.

   B Your teacher will has answered that question often.

8. **A** Loren will have read the play before she went to sleep last night.

   B Loren had read the play before she went to sleep last night.

9. **A** I have been invited to Sue's party next Saturday.

   B I have invited to Sue's party next Saturday.

10. **A** JoAnn had gotten her mom's approval before she went to New York.

    B JoAnn will have gotten her mom's approval before she went to New York.

◆C Apply

Change the tense of the verb in each sentence to the form in parentheses.
Rewrite the new sentence on the line.

1. My sons <u>ate</u> the whole pizza. (present perfect)

   _____

2. A mouse <u>lived</u> in my wall for months. (present perfect)

   _____

3. Next week, Gina <u>will bike</u> to work five times. (future perfect)

   _____

4. I did not know that you <u>wanted</u> a ticket, too. (past perfect)

   _____

Complete each sentence with a form of the verb in parentheses. Use present
perfect, past perfect, or future perfect tense. The underlined words and
phrases are clues.

5. (type) Mike _____ most of his paper <u>before his</u>

   <u>computer crashed</u>.

6. (cough) Several people in the audience _____ <u>through</u>

   <u>the whole show</u>.

7. (eat) Local farmers fear that grasshoppers _____ all the wheat

   <u>before harvest this fall</u>.

8. (save) <u>By next year</u> Lisa _____ enough for a used car.

9. (run) Although Lester _____ for almost every office in town,

   he <u>is still looking</u> for his first victory.

10. (drive) <u>Before they ran out of gas</u>, the car thieves _____ around

    aimlessly.

D Check Up

Circle the letter of the verb that best completes each sentence.

1. By the end of this double bill, Craig _____ eight movies this week.

   A will have seeing

   B will have seen

   C will have been seen

   D sees

2. Hailey drove home after she _____ her flat tire.

   F has changed

   G had changed

   H will have changed

   J have change

3. By the time the train arrived at the station, many passengers _____ friends.

   A will become

   B will have become

   C have became

   D had become

4. Since I dropped the mouse, the computer _____ well.

   F has not worked

   G will not have worked

   H has not work

   J have not worked

Read the sentences below, paying special attention to verbs and their tenses. Circle the letter of the sentence that is written correctly.

5. **A** Until he turned three, my brother had not begun to talk.

   B Long before he was born, there has been a quiet president.

   C When Calvin Coolidge was in the White House, people been calling him "Silent Cal."

   D Until my brother started to talk, my dad calls him "Silent Cal."

6. **F** The people of Livermore have being proud of a particular light bulb.

   G Before World War II began, this light bulb had burned for years.

   H Today it shines in the fire department and tourists had come to see it.

   J We wonder how long it will have been shined before it burns out.

7. **A** Phones changes much since people first used them.

   B Around 1920 only a few homes on each block have had a phone.

   C At that time, people down the block will have used a neighbor's phone.

   D Today people carry phones in their pockets on walks down the block.

Agreement of Subjects and Verbs

Present tense verbs change form to show number.
The **plural form** of a verb is its base form. It does not
end in *-s*. Use the plural form of a verb with a plural subject.

> Birdwatchers <u>look</u> for unusual birds.

> We <u>enjoy</u> the challenge.

Also use the plural form of a verb with *I* and *you*.

> I <u>meet</u> nice people on bird walks.

> You <u>see</u> more birds with help from others.

The **singular form** of almost every verb is its base form plus *-s* or *-es*. Use the singular form of a verb with a third-person singular subject. (A subject is third-person singular if you can replace it with *he, she,* or *it*.)

> Every birdwatcher <u>looks</u> for unusual birds.

> Nobody <u>enjoys</u> a challenge more than Joe <u>does</u>.

Here are the important exceptions to the above rules:

- The plural form of *be* is *are* (*we are, you are, they are*).

- *Be* has two singular forms, *am* and *is*. Use *am* with *I* (*I am*). Use *is* with *he, she,* and *it* (*he is, she is, it is*).

- The singular form of the verb *have* is *has* (*he, she,* or *it has*). The plural form is *have* (*we have, they have*).

Underline the subject and the correct verb form in parentheses. On the line, write S if the verb is singular or P if the verb is plural.

1. _____ My son (sells, sell) insurance.

2. _____ These flowers (blooms, bloom) in fall.

3. _____ The art museum (opens, open) at 11:00.

4. _____ Most clubs (charges, charge) dues.

5. _____ I (am, is, are) on my way to the store.

6. _____ Weather forecasters (uses, use) the latest information.

7. _____ Crows (has, have) a harsh call.

8. _____ Which truck (carries, carry) the most cargo?

B ▶ Practice

In many sentences, a phrase comes between the subject and the verb. Be sure to choose the verb form that agrees with the subject rather than the last word in the phrase.

> <u>Each</u> of those singers <u>is</u> very loud. (The subject is *each*, a singular pronoun. The verb must be singular.)

> <u>Members</u> of the band <u>are</u> on stage. (The subject is *members*, a plural noun. The verb must be plural.)

If you are not sure whether a verb should be singular or plural, first find the subject. In your mind, erase any words between the subject and the verb. Then it will be easier to choose the right verb form.

> **Problem:** Teens in the audience (loves, love) this music.

> **Process:** The subject is the plural noun, *Teens*. Think of the sentence as Teens ~~in the audience~~ (loves, love) this music.

> **Solution:** <u>Teens</u> in the audience <u>love</u> this music.

In each sentence, circle the subject. Draw a line through any phrase between the subject and verb. Then underline the correct verb form.

1. The temperature on the islands (varies, vary) only a few degrees year-round.

2. Most kindergartners, after a short nap, (has, have) a burst of energy.

3. Lawyers for the defendant (presents, present) their case today.

4. The leader of the rebels (claims, claim) to be the country's lawful ruler.

5. Dotie's favorite machine among all her appliances (am, is, are) the toaster.

6. Announcers on this station (seems, seem) to enjoy their jobs.

7. Almost every day, noises from the street (keeps, keep) my baby awake.

8. The ramps at the next interchange (am, is, are) being repaved this month.

9. The worst score of any student in both classes (am, is, are) only a C.

10. A mother of twins (needs, need) extra arms.

11. Many travelers on their way to the historic site (stops, stop) at this small store to buy snacks.

A compound subject has two or more parts. If the parts of the subject are joined by *and*, use a plural verb.

> The team's <u>owner</u> and the <u>manager</u> <u>agree</u> on most issues.

If the parts of a compound subject are joined by *or* or *nor*, the verb should agree with the part closest to the verb.

> Either the young <u>manager</u> or the older <u>coaches</u> <u>give</u> advice to players. (The plural subject *coaches* is closer to the verb, so the verb is plural.)

> Neither the old <u>coaches</u> nor the young <u>manager</u> <u>does</u> everything perfectly. (The singular subject *manager* is closer to the verb, so the verb is singular.)

In each sentence, underline each part of the compound subject and circle the word (*and*, *or*, or *nor*) joining the parts. Then underline the correct verb form in parentheses.

1. Neither my daughter nor her friends (has, have) commented on the new computers at school.

2. The yellow curtains and the flowered bedspread (needs, need) to be cleaned.

3. Either rabbits or a deer (eats, eat) the vegetables in the garden each night.

4. Both Antoine and Leo (knows, know) the combination to this lock.

5. Three cars or one bus (fills, fill) the tiny parking lot behind the school.

Complete each sentence by writing the correct form of the verb in parentheses.

6. (worry) Alicia and Tom _____ about everything.

7. (cause) Heavy rains or fog _____ at least one accident per week on these mountain roads.

8. (hold) The locked box or these coded messages _____ the answer to the mystery.

9. (take) The boys and their father _____ long bike rides every weekend.

10. (be) Neither the stars nor the sun _____ made of solid matter.

Circle the letter of the verb that best completes each sentence.

1. This car _____ high ratings for safety.

   A receive

   B are receiving

   C have received

   D has received

2. Strawberries or a banana _____ Sally an upset stomach.

   F gives

   G give

   H have given

   J are giving

3. One shipment of books _____ about 1,000 pounds.

   A have weighed

   B weighs

   C are weighing

   D weigh

4. The kittens and their mother _____ with the yarn.

   F plays

   G has played

   H play

   J is playing

Read the sentences below. Circle the letter of the sentence in which the subject and verb agree.

5. A I is not willing to go to an amusement park on a hot day.

   B The high temperature or the wild rides makes me feel sick.

   C A scary roller coaster, even on cool days, upsets my stomach.

6. F Wu, one of my old friends, want a new car.

   G Her old car have been giving her troubles lately.

   H Neither luxury cars nor a van is in Wu's budget.

7. A Does you want to go out to lunch today?

   B Both coffee shops in our building provide fast service.

   C One of the burgers are what I usually order.

8. F The specials at this sale is worth considering.

   G Three waste baskets or one paper shredder costs ten dollars.

   H Many regular customers and at least one newcomer is browsing.

Adjectives

Adjectives are words that describe nouns and pronouns.
They tell *what kind*, *how many*, or *how much*.

> <u>Four</u> (*how many*) men squeezed into that
> <u>small green</u> (*what kind*) car.

Adjectives can be used to compare two or more things.
If the adjective has only one or two syllables, add *–er* to
compare two things. This is called the **comparative form**.
Add *–est* to compare three or more things. This is called
the **superlative form**.

> **Comparative:** Monday was <u>warmer</u> than Tuesday. (compares *Monday*
> and *Tuesday*)

> **Superlative:** Monday was the <u>warmest</u> day this week. (compares
> *Monday* and all of the other days of the week)

If the adjective has two or more syllables, use the words **more** or **less** to
compare two things. Use the words **most** or **least** to compare three or more
things.

> My car is <u>more expensive</u> than this one.

> Your car is the <u>most expensive</u> of the three.

Use only one form of an adjective in a comparison.

> **Wrong:** This loaf of bread is <u>more fresher</u> than that loaf.

> **Right:** This loaf of bread is <u>fresher</u> than that loaf.

Underline every adjective in each sentence.

1. The old apple tree was covered with pink blossoms.

2. Soon bright green leaves appeared on each branch.

3. Is a collie bigger than a bulldog?

4. A noisy crowd cheered in the new sports arena.

5. The snowy Alps are the largest range of mountains in Europe.

6. This is the most delicious hamburger I've ever tasted!

7. She put on a long woolen coat and warm mittens.

8. Was the score on the last test higher than on the first one?

B Practice

Before adding *–er* or *–est* to an adjective, follow these rules:

- If the adjective has one syllable, a short vowel, and a single consonant at the end, double the final consonant.
  fa<u>t</u> → fa<u>tt</u>er
- If the adjective ends in *e*, drop the final *e*.
  humbl<u>e</u> → humblest
- If the adjective ends in a consonant and *y*, change the *y* to *i*.
  shin<u>y</u> → shin<u>i</u>er

A few adjectives do not follow the usual pattern. In these comparisons, the whole word changes.

good → better → best   bad → worse → worst

many → more → most   little → less → least

Fill in the boxes with the correct form of each adjective.

	Adjective	Comparative Form	Superlative Form
1.	early		
2.			fewest
3.		wetter	
4.			most quiet
5.		less expensive	
6.		better	
7.	large		

Read each sentence. If the underlined adjective is not correct, write the proper form on the line. If there is no mistake, write *Correct*.

8. Mowing grass is <u>more harder</u> than trimming shrubs. _____

9. Did you bring the <u>thinnest</u> wire you could find? _____

10. Her latest movie was <u>more worse</u> than the one before it. _____

11. My friend carried the <u>heavy</u> box to my house. _____

C ▸ Apply

On each line, write two adjectives to describe each noun.

1. _____ _____ horse

2. _____ _____ lake

3. _____ _____ stone

4. _____ _____ book

5. _____ _____ job

6. _____ _____ quarterback

7. _____ _____ cook

8. _____ _____ adventure

Use the adjective in parentheses to complete each sentence. Use the correct form when comparing two or more things.

9. (fast) Stan ran the _____ time of all the runners in the race.

10. (short) That table leg looks _____ than the other one.

11. (delicious) As a judge at the fair, Amos chose the _____ pie in the contest.

12. (large) Is a cheetah or a lion the _____ animal?

13. (tasty) Cherry tomatoes are _____ than grape tomatoes.

14. (beautiful) Do the Smiths or the Johnsons have the _____ backyard?

15. (ripe) Of these three melons, which one is the _____?

16. (bright) Sirius is the _____ star in the sky.

Circle the adjective that correctly completes the sentence.

1. Take the _____ of the four books to the library.

    A biggest

    B bigger

    C more big

    D most biggest

2. I always do the _____ of all my chores first.

    F importantest

    G more importanter

    H most important

    J important

3. Mike is _____ when baseball season starts.

    A most happiest

    B happy

    C happyest

    D more happier

4. We saw a _____ sunset last evening.

    F beautiful

    G more beautiful

    H most beautiful

    J more beautifuller

5. Jeremy turned the volume to a _____ setting than before.

    A loud

    B more loud

    C louder

    D loudder

6. This is the _____ mess I've ever seen!

    F baddest

    G most bad

    H worse

    J worst

7. This cream paint is a _____ color than the beige paint.

    A more lighter

    B lightest

    C light

    D lighter

8. I overslept this morning and caught a _____ train than usual.

    F more late

    G later

    H latter

    J more later

Adverbs

Adverbs are used to add meaning to verbs. They tell *how, when, where,* or *to what degree.* Many adverbs end in *-ly.*

> My dog <u>always</u> barks at trucks. (when)
>
> My dog barks <u>loudly</u> at trucks. (how)

In comparisons, adverbs follow the same pattern as adjectives. If an adverb is short, add *-er* to compare two actions. Add *-est* to compare three or more actions.

> The drug store closes <u>later</u> than the shoe store.
>
> Of all the mall stores, the barber shop closes <u>latest</u>.

If the adverb has at least two syllables, use **more** or **less** when comparing two actions. Use **most** or **least** when comparing more than two actions.

> Eliza sews <u>less often</u> than Marie.
>
> Of all the club members, Vanessa sews <u>least often</u>.

Find the adverb in each sentence, and write it on the line.

1. We carefully walked up the creaky stairs. _____

2. I never expected to become a good cook. _____

3. Ricardo went home early because he finished the job. _____

4. Bees buzzed busily in the flowerbeds. _____

5. The river runs rapidly near the bottom of the hill. _____

6. Fishing season started yesterday. _____

7. I already sent the package to her. _____

8. Hummingbirds fly faster than blue jays. _____

9. They slowly climbed to the top of the hill. _____

10. He arrived sooner than we thought he would. _____

When adding *–er* or *–est* to an adverb to form a comparison, follow the same spelling rules as for adjectives.

Tom came <u>late</u>. I came <u>later</u>. Nancy came <u>latest</u> of all. (*late, later, latest*)

Jo came <u>early</u>. I came <u>earlier</u>. Tia came <u>earliest</u> of all. (*early, earlier, earliest*)

Some adverbs follow a special form for comparisons.

well → better → best   badly → worse → worst
much → more → most   little → less → least

Remember to use just one form of the adverb in a comparison.

Wrong: He arrived <u>more sooner</u> than I did.

Right: He arrived <u>sooner</u> than I did.

Write each adverb under the correct heading.

almost   worst   more rapidly   most gladly   earliest
now   nearer   well   more clearly

Adverbs	Comparative Forms	Superlative Forms
1. _____	4. _____	7. _____
2. _____	5. _____	8. _____
3. _____	6. _____	9. _____

Find the adverb in each sentence. If the form is wrong, write it correctly on the line. If there are no mistakes, write *Correct*.

10. He swam the most farthest of his squad. _____

11. Trena practiced most better than she did yesterday. _____

12. The turtles moved slowest along the beach. _____

13. The job is nearly done. _____

14. They more easily helped us find our lost package. _____

15. We barely saw the stop sign through the fog. _____

C Apply

Write an adverb on each line that describes *how*, *when*, or *where* the action takes place.

1. gallop _____

2. drift _____

3. work _____

4. decide _____

5. glow _____

Complete each sentence by adding an adverb. Use the proper form for any comparison.

6. Listen _____ to learn what you are to do.

7. The stray cat _____ scratched my hand.

8. Rosa paints _____ than I do.

9. Victor _____ uses his computer to send e-mail.

10. Please give me your answer _____.

11. Does the snack bar open _____ than the restaurant?

12. Sean climbed the steep hill _____.

13. The man yelled _____ when he fell out of the boat.

14. I am not interested in buying any jewelry _____.

15. Team A exercises _____ of all the teams at the gym.

◆D◆ Check Up

Circle the adverb that correctly completes the sentence.

1. All the dancers moved _____ to the music.

   A more smoother

   B smooth

   C smoothly

   D smoothest

2. She played the sport very _____.

   F well

   G good

   H best

   J better

3. The fire spread _____ through the house.

   A most quick

   B quickly

   C quicklier

   D more quickly

4. Can't you walk any _____ than that?

   F more faster

   G fastest

   H fast

   J faster

5. Stir the soup _____ so it does not splash on you.

   A slowly

   B more slower

   C most slowly

   D slowest

6. They _____ lifted the heavy sod off the truck.

   F easier

   G easily

   H more easy

   J most easily

7. Phil plays drums _____ than his brother does.

   A more good

   B more better

   C gooder

   D better

8. My dog _____ cut his paw.

   F bad

   G badly

   H more badly

   J worst

A Introduce

Adjective or Adverb?

Both adjectives and adverbs describe other words. Sometimes the same word is used as an adjective in one sentence and as an adverb in another.

> This is a <u>fast</u> horse. (adjective)
> The horse walked <u>fast</u>. (adverb)

For the adjective *good* and the adverb *well*, the forms used in comparisons look the same:

adjective: good   better   best
adverb: well   better   best

Here are some ways to tell the difference between an adjective and an adverb.

Adjectives	Adverbs
• describe nouns or pronouns	• describe verbs
• tell *what kind, how many,* or *how much*	• tell *how, when, where,* or *to what degree*
	• many, but not all, end in *-ly*

Read each sentence. Write on the line whether the underlined word is an *adjective* or an *adverb*.

1. <u>Several</u> people fainted from the heat. _____

2. <u>Quickly</u> decide if you are coming with us. _____

3. We skated <u>skillfully</u> through the crowd. _____

4. That project was done <u>yesterday</u>. _____

5. I <u>never</u> tell my age to anyone. _____

6. Everyone enjoyed the <u>wonderful</u> meal. _____

7. The stars are <u>bright</u> tonight. _____

8. She hummed the new song <u>softly</u> to herself. _____

9. Catch the <u>early</u> bus if you want a seat. _____

10. We left the party <u>early</u>. _____

B ▶ Practice

Many adjectives that tell *what kind* are changed to adverbs that tell *how* by the addition of *-ly*. Here are some examples:

Adjective	Adverb
cool	coolly
happy	happily
even	evenly

When these adjectives and adverbs are used in comparisons, their forms have clear differences. Study these examples:

Adjective	Adverb
cool, cooler, coolest	coolly, more coolly, most coolly
happy, happier, happiest	happily, more happily, most happily
even, more even, most even	evenly, more evenly, most evenly

Be sure to decide whether an adjective or an adverb is needed before choosing the correct form of the word.

Circle the correct form of the adjective or adverb in each sentence.

1. One headlight is (more brightly, brighter) than the other.

2. The police officer spoke (kindly, kind) to the child.

3. Summer is our (busiest, most busily) season of the year.

4. You are the (most nicely, nicest) man I know.

5. On dress-down day, staff members dress (more casual, more casually) than on other days.

6. The manager gave a (well, good) reason for the new rules.

7. This is the (most expensive, most expensively) outfit I own.

8. Who works (quieter, more quietly), Ned or Al?

9. Our efforts produced a (good, well) outcome.

10. This book is much (more interesting, more interestingly) than the last one by this writer.

11. The students walked (swift, swiftly) down the street.

C Apply

Use an adjective or an adverb from the box to complete each sentence.
Change the word to its comparative or superlative form as needed.

careful	easy	attractive
	eagerly	deeply

1. Every _____ driver makes sure that his or her passengers

   buckle up.

2. This job is definitely _____than my last one.

3. After their father offered a prize, the children did their chores

   _____.

4. The rose garden is a _____ area than the lawn.

5. The singer was _____ hurt by the audience's reaction.

In each sentence, use the correct adjective or adverb form of a word in the box.

calm	immediate
happy	deeply	young

6. A sheep dog is _____ than a greyhound.

7. The medic _____ ran to help the injured man.

8. All the winners waved _____ to the crowd.

9. Who is the _____ of your four friends?

10. Did you finish this job _____ than the other one?

◆D Check Up

Read the sentences below. Circle the letter of the sentence with the correct form of the adjective or adverb.

1. **A** That is a slowly train.

   B That is a more slow train.

   C That train moves slowly.

   D That train moves slowest.

2. **F** Maya Angelou is a good known poet.

   G Maya Angelou is a goodly known poet.

   H Many people speak highly of her poetry.

   J Many people speak high of her poetry.

3. **A** What a quick job you did!

   B My pet learns quick.

   C He learns more quicker than any other pet I've owned.

   D You do the most quickly work of anybody.

4. **F** Grace plays baseball very skillful.

   G Grace is skillfuller than her teammates.

   H She caught the fast ball more skillful.

   J She skillfully caught the fast ball.

Look at the underlined word or words in each sentence. Choose the answer that is written correctly for the underlined part.

5. The wolf <u>hungrily</u> eyed his prey.

   A more hungrily

   B hungriest

   C hungrier

   D Correct as it is

6. Speak <u>truthful</u> if you want to be trusted.

   F truthfullest

   G more truthful

   H truthfully

   J Correct as it is

7. He is the <u>handsomer</u> person at the party.

   A most handsomely

   B most handsome

   C most handsomest

   D Correct as it is

8. Miles sorted the papers <u>more careful</u> than Nelson did.

   F carefuller

   G more carefully

   H carefully

   J Correct as it is

A Introduce

Using Negative Words

Some people use two negative words in the same clause or sentence. That practice is called using a **double negative**. In certain situations, such as at work, using double negatives is nonstandard. It is not accepted in formal discussions or in writing.

To correct a double negative, take away one of the negative words.

> **Double negative:** Sue did<u>n't</u> get <u>no</u> invitation to the party.

> **Standard:**   Sue did<u>n't</u> get <u>any</u> invitation to the party.

> **Standard:**   Sue got <u>no</u> invitation to the party.

Here is a list of common negative words:

never	no	none	not
nothing	nobody	no one	nowhere

Remember that contractions that end in *-n't* are negative words. They should not be used together with the negative words listed above. The words *hardly* and *barely* are also negative words.

> **Double negative:** I ca<u>n't</u> <u>hardly</u> see the screen.

> **Standard:**   I can <u>hardly</u> see the screen.

> **Standard:**   I ca<u>n't</u> <u>see</u> the screen well.

Write *DN* if the sentence has a double negative. Write *S* before each sentence that uses negative words in a standard way.

1. _____ The bus doesn't stop here no more.

2. _____ I didn't ask for none of these onions on my hot dog.

3. _____ Lila didn't know hardly anyone at the meeting.

4. _____ No one else had a problem with the directions.

5. _____ Bill never asks for no help with his work.

6. _____ Nobody is getting in without no ticket.

7. _____ I was so tired I could barely get up this morning.

8. _____ The neighbors hadn't seen nothing strange that night.

9. _____ There wasn't anything missing from the locker.

B ▶ Practice

Circle the word that completes each sentence correctly.

1. Jess hasn't (never, ever) seen that TV show.

2. Emma (had, hadn't) been here barely five minutes before she left.

3. Don't give Tim (no, any) peanut butter.

4. Wes doesn't listen to (no, any) jazz.

5. I offered her some dessert, but she didn't want (any, none).

6. Can't (anybody, nobody) reach the top shelf?

7. Paul couldn't find his favorite cap (nowhere, anywhere).

8. Sara (could, couldn't) hardly speak above a whisper.

9. There wasn't (nothing, anything) you could have done.

10. Didn't (any, none) of you get my joke?

Each first sentence has a double negative. Circle the letter of the sentence that corrects the double negative.

11. Won't no one ever make a good low-fat cheesecake?

   A Won't anyone never make a good low-fat cheesecake?

   B Won't anyone ever make a good low-fat cheesecake?

12. James didn't want nobody to read his poem.

   A James didn't want anybody to read his poem.

   B James wanted hardly nobody to read his poem.

13. The missing puzzle piece wasn't nowhere to be found.

   A The missing puzzle piece was nowhere to be found.

   B The missing puzzle piece couldn't be found nowhere.

14. I didn't get nothing in the mail today.

   A I didn't get hardly anything in the mail today.

   B I got nothing in the mail today.

C Apply

If the sentence contains a double negative, rewrite it correctly on the line. If it uses negative words in a standard way, write *Correct*.

1. Kevin couldn't hardly wait until the weekend.

   _____

2. There isn't no one who blames you for the accident.

   _____

3. Alex hasn't ever visited Alaska.

   _____

4. Can't nobody tell me who won the game?

   _____

5. My dog doesn't never come when I call.

   _____

6. There wasn't barely enough popcorn for the whole family.

   _____

7. The pilot hadn't said nothing about having a problem.

   _____

8. Nobody ever plays that song anymore.

   _____

9. I never asked for no favors, and I don't expect none.

   _____

10. I didn't see your cell phone nowhere in the house.

   _____

D Check Up

Read each set of sentences below. Choose the sentence that uses negative words correctly.

1. **A** Dan hasn't had no colds.

   B Don't you ever knock before you come into a room?

   C Nobody has no idea where she went.

   D Beth didn't learn nothing from the salesclerk.

2. **F** I could barely hear him.

   G The little boat couldn't hardly make it through the storm.

   H Won't nobody please turn down that radio?

   J Olive couldn't find no dimes for the parking meter.

3. **A** No one was expecting no problems today.

   B Didn't you never make any mistakes yourself?

   C My parents didn't allow no singing at the dinner table.

   D Was nothing ever bought to replace this old washer?

4. **F** We haven't gone nowhere.

   G Anne doesn't like no tea.

   H We barely made it home before the rain started.

   J The mayor hasn't done nothing about the crime in our city.

Read each sentence and look at the underlined words. Choose the answer that is written correctly for the underlined words.

5. Unless you bring in a coupon, you <u>won't get no</u> money off your purchase.

   A won't get any

   B won't never get

   C will never get no

   D Correct as it is

6. I <u>didn't hardly know</u> when you would get back from your trip.

   F didn't never know

   G didn't have no idea

   H didn't know

   J Correct as it is

7. We <u>haven't hired no one</u> for that job yet, but we will keep you in mind.

   A haven't done no hiring

   B haven't hired anybody

   C haven't hired nobody

   D Correct as it is

8. I <u>never got any</u> flowers for my birthday before!

   F never got no

   G didn't ever get no

   H didn't never get any

   J Correct as it is

Nouns

A **noun** names a person, place, or thing. Nouns can be singular or plural. They can be common or proper. Capitalize all the words in a proper noun.

Pronouns

A **pronoun** is a word used in place of a noun. Pronouns must agree with their antecedents in gender, number, and person.

Verbs

A verb is a word that names an action or a state of being. There are **action verbs, linking verbs,** and **helping verbs.** Verbs change form to show when the action that is described happens. These forms are called **tenses.** Verbs change form to agree with a singular or a plural subject.

Adjectives and Adverbs

Adjectives are words that add meaning to nouns and pronouns. They tell *what kind, how many,* or *how much.* **Adverbs** add meaning to verbs. They tell *how, when, where,* or *to what degree.* Many adverbs end in *-ly.* Adjectives and adverbs change their forms when they are used to compare things or actions.

Using Negatives

In formal situations avoid using two negative words in the same clause or sentence. Negative words include the following: *no, not, never, nothing, nowhere, nobody, hardly, barely,* and all contractions made using the word *not.*

Choose the word that correctly completes each sentence.

1. Send your payment to _____.

   A we

   B I

   C us

   D our

2. The employees _____ will decide who will lead them.

   F them

   G themselves

   H herself

   J theirself

3. The tree _____ my father planted is now 30 feet tall.

   A that

   B whom

   C whose

   D who

4. Ed _____ two dozen cookies.

   F is bake

   G baked

   H baking

   J are baking

5. Last year we _____ to Europe.

   A are traveling

   B traveling

   C will travel

   D traveled

6. One guest _____ his coat.

   F leaving

   G have left

   H has left

   J is left

7. The movers have _____ all the furniture into the house.

   A bring

   B brought

   C bringed

   D bringing

8. Why don't you pick up the _____ of the three boxes?

   F most lightest

   G more lighter

   H lighter

   J lightest

9. My cat eats _____ than my dog.

   A delicately

   B more delicately

   C most delicately

   D more delicatelier

10. Watch your diet _____.

   F carefully

   G most careful

   H more carefuller

   J careful

11. **A** Didn't no one pack matches?

   B Last year, your garden didn't never look this beautiful.

   C I could hardly finish my meal at that restaurant.

   D Don't leave no personal belongings behind.

12. **F** When Dave gets to Austin, him will send me a postcard.

   G Have you forgotten mine birthday again?

   H Cassie gave herself a pep talk before the interview.

   J Stack them books next to the computer.

13. **A** Years from now, we will look back at today and laugh.

   B Last night I will wait for you for an hour.

   C Right now I am want a cold drink.

   D Josh was made the dessert last night.

14. **F** The farmer has a difficult job.

   G When it rains too much, farmers were not able to plant.

   H Farmers will waiting for a good day to plant.

   J When city folks are playing, the farmers were at work.

15. **A** U.S. bills changing their look.

   B Criminals have found it too easy to copy them.

   C Agents has caught many counterfeiters.

   D Someday the new bills will be seemed familiar.

16. **F** This mountain is tall than that one.

   G If you see a better deal, take it.

   H This box of berries seems more fresher than that one.

   J Eric has proved that he is the most fastest runner of all.

17. **A** Eliza played the waltz more slower than usual.

   B Of the three, Jackie dances better.

   C Yvette beat the old record easilier than we expected.

   D The birds seem to start singing earlier every day.

18. **F** Your car has a quietly engine.

   G Play quietly while the baby is sleeping.

   H We tried to walk quiet when we came late to the meeting.

   J You speak too soft for me to hear you.

◆ Assessment *continued*

Read the passages and look at the underlined parts. Choose the answer that is written correctly for each underlined part.

(19)   When Julie moved to her new home, she <u>take</u> her cat along. She
(20) thought the cat would adjust to their new home. But the cat <u>missed</u>
(21) the old home. One day Julie let her cat out, and it <u>didn't never</u>
(22) come back. Julie still waits for <u>their</u> cat to come back. From now on,
she will be more careful about letting her pets out.

19. A taken   **21. F** didn't hardly
     B taking   **G** couldn't never
     C took   **H** didn't ever
     D Correct as it is   **J** Correct as it is

20. F miss   **22. A** its
     G will miss   **B** her
     H have missed   **C** our
     J Correct as it is   **D** Correct as it is

     Have you ever heard of the Pony Express? In 1860 business
(23) leaders <u>hire</u> young men to carry mail on horseback across the
(24) wilderness. Only <u>skillful</u> and brave riders got the jobs. For 18 months,
(25) the riders did their jobs well. They <u>didn't lose hardly any</u> mail
on their dangerous cross-country rides. Then telegraph wires were
strung across the country. Riders discovered that no one needed
(26) <u>his</u> service anymore. The Pony Express went out of business.

23. F have hired   **25. F** didn't lose barely any
     G hires   **G** lost hardly any
     H hired   **H** didn't lose no
     J Correct as it is   **J** Correct as it is

24. A skillfuller   **26. A** their
     B more skillful   **B** your
     C most skillfullest   **C** her
     D Correct as it is   **D** Correct as it is

Complete Sentences and Fragments

To speak and write clearly, use complete sentences. A complete sentence has both a subject and a predicate. The **subject** is the person or thing that is doing something. The **predicate** tells what the subject is doing. The predicate includes a verb and other words that tell about the verb.

> The rodeo champ <u>fell</u> off his horse.

> *The rodeo champ* is the subject, and *fell off his horse* is the predicate. The simple subject is *champ*. The verb is *fell*.

A **fragment** is not a complete sentence. The following are descriptions and examples of two common types of sentence fragments:

1. Fragments may have a subject but no predicate.

   Fragment: Stars in the midnight sky.

   Complete sentence: Stars in the midnight sky <u>shone brightly</u>. (Add a predicate.)

2. Fragments may have a predicate but no subject.

   Fragment: Wrote a poem about her father.

   Complete sentence: <u>Angela</u> wrote a poem about her father. (Add a subject.)

Write *CS* beside each complete sentence. Underline its subject and circle its predicate. Write *F* beside each fragment.

1. _____ Sang along with the radio.

2. _____ Aunt Zelda loves country music.

3. _____ My cat broke the lamp.

4. _____ Took my cat for a walk.

5. _____ The dog in my neighbor's yard.

6. _____ The drug store on Elm Street.

7. _____ Howl at the moon all night.

8. _____ The baby in the stroller was hungry.

9. _____ A car drove up to the house.

When it stands alone, a fragment does not make sense. Something is missing.

Fragment: Under the back porch

Fragment: Although it looked great on her

Sometimes a fragment belongs with the sentence before or after it.

Fragment: Although it looked great on her. Maria didn't buy the sweater.

Corrected: Although it looked great on her, Maria didn't buy the sweater.

Fragment: The cat had her kittens. Under the back porch.

Corrected: The cat had her kittens under the back porch.

Write *CS* beside each complete sentence. Write *F* beside each fragment. If the fragment can be corrected by connecting it to another sentence, put a circle around the sentence and fragment.

1. _____ Unless it begins to rain. In the morning.

2. _____ We looked outside at the hail. Falling hard, like thousands of pebbles.

3. _____ The rain is running down the windowpane.

4. _____ Flies swarm around the garbage.

5. _____ Laughing and making jokes.

6. _____ Luis has a dental appointment. In an hour.

7. _____ At the table for two by the window.

8. _____ Our waiter knocked the glass over.

9. _____ You will have good luck. If you throw salt over your left shoulder.

10. _____ Because it has chocolate in it.

11. _____ The candle on the table. Was dripping hot wax.

12. _____ The girls were playing basketball.

13. _____ While we were standing on the corner.

14. _____ I found my pen. On the table next to the phone.

C Apply

Read each of the fragments below. Correct each fragment by turning it into a complete sentence. Write the sentences on the lines.

1. Into the ball park.

   _____

2. The coach at third base.

   _____

3. Evelyn should be a teacher. Because she likes children.

   _____

4. Ran in a 10K race over the weekend.

   _____

5. Until yesterday. I thought that Travis and Pete were brothers.

   _____

6. Janet is bringing her baseball glove. Thinks she'll catch a fly ball.

   _____

7. We sang the anthem. With our hands over our hearts.

   _____

8. Playing the toughest team in the league.

   _____

9. Bought a new CD at the record store.

   _____

10. We sat on the beach. As the sun set.

    _____

D Check Up

For each item, circle the letter of the complete sentence.

1. A At four o'clock every day.

   B The screeching bats at night.

   C Some cats have six toes on each paw.

   D Although the dog is friendly.

2. F Because she is older than he is.

   G Tamika finished the ice cream last night.

   H Drives a baby-blue Cougar.

   J A tattoo of an eagle on his arm.

3. A The bus is due at five P.M.

   B With a glass of orange juice.

   C Closed for the season.

   D The shade beneath the maple tree.

4. F A bunch of green bananas.

   G Because I told the secret.

   H Drove across the Golden Gate Bridge.

   J Her favorite ride is the roller coaster.

Read the passage and look at the underlined parts. Choose the answer that is written correctly for each underlined part.

(5)   Boston's Fenway Park. Is one of the oldest major league baseball parks in America. It opened back in 1912. Fenway Park has many features that make it special. The 37-foot-high left field wall is known as

(6)   "The Green Monster." Many of baseball's most famous players called Fenway home. Including Cy Young, Babe Ruth, and Ted Williams. Nearly a century old, Fenway Park is a link to baseball history.

5. A Boston's Fenway Park is one of the oldest major league baseball parks in America.

   B Boston's Fenway Park is. One of the oldest major league baseball parks in America.

   C Boston's Fenway Park is one of the oldest major league baseball parks. In America.

   D Correct as it is

6. F Many of baseball's most famous players. Called Fenway home, including Cy Young, Babe Ruth, and Ted Williams.

   G Many of baseball's most famous players called Fenway home, including Cy Young, Babe Ruth, and Ted Williams.

   H Many of baseball's most famous players. Called Fenway home, including Cy Young. Babe Ruth and Ted Williams.

   J Correct as it is

Run-On Sentences

It is important to avoid run-on sentences when you write. **Run-on sentences** combine two or more sentences without proper punctuation. Readers don't know where one idea ends and the next begins.

In some run-on sentences, two sentences are joined with no punctuation between them. To correct these run-ons, split the sentence in two. Add an end mark to the first sentence. Begin the second sentence with a capital letter.

Run-on: Mark didn't get home until eight o'clock he was busy at work.

Correct: Mark didn't get home until eight o'clock. He was busy at work.

In other run-on sentences, a comma is used to join two sentences. One way to correct this kind of run-on is to split the sentence into two sentences. Another way is to add a conjunction such as *and*, *but*, or *or* after the comma.

Run-on: Jeannie loves all kinds of music, her favorite style is jazz.

Correct: Jeannie loves all kinds of music. Her favorite style is jazz.

Correct: Jeannie loves all kinds of music, but her favorite style is jazz.

Write *CS* beside each complete sentence and *RO* beside each run-on sentence.

1. _____ Matt and Yoko took a drive they went out to the country.

2. _____ You can buy blueberries, but the strawberries look fresher.

3. _____ She doesn't want to live on a farm, she'd miss the city.

4. _____ You can see more stars in the country.

5. _____ The roads are spooky at night there are no streetlights.

6. _____ Shannon likes to sit on her fire escape at night.

7. _____ We know the man who owns the store, his name is Delroy.

8. _____ This house was built in 1800, a famous writer lived there.

9. _____ Jim writes poems about rivers he used to be a river guide.

10. _____ The theatre is closed this week.

Identify each word group below as a complete sentence (*CS*), a fragment (*F*), or a run-on (*RO*).

1. _____ Thomas joined the navy he loves ships.

2. _____ It isn't safe to drive that car because its radiator leaks.

3. _____ Saw a good movie on Friday night.

4. _____ Shari is next you're after Shari.

5. _____ It's raining you should take an umbrella.

6. _____ Wanted to go swimming at the lake.

7. _____ Pedro will drive, he knows the way.

8. _____ Belinda has a car, but it is not running.

9. _____ I would like to swim I need to borrow a towel.

10. _____ In the deep part of the lake.

11. _____ Tina wants to see Star Wars, she's seen it five times already.

12. _____ Charles might need some help that couch looks heavy.

13. _____ Ana will be in Mexico until next April.

14. _____ A light snow beginning to fall.

15. _____ She speaks Spanish he does not.

Read the following pairs of sentences. Circle the letter of the sentence in each pair that is correct.

16. **A** The morning had been cloudy, but the sky cleared by noon.

    B The morning had been cloudy the sky cleared by noon.

17. **A** Linda enjoys puzzles she always does the Sunday crossword puzzle.

    B Linda enjoys puzzles. She always does the Sunday crossword puzzle.

18. **A** Mike found a good deal for a car on the Internet.

    B Mike found a good deal. For a car on the Internet.

C ◆ Apply

Decide if each word group is a complete sentence or a run-on. If it is a complete sentence, write *CS* on the line. If it is a run-on, correct it.

1. Tara has a new baby it's a girl.

   _____

2. Spike left town, I haven't seen him in days.

   _____

3. This coffee is weak I'll make some more.

   _____

4. We went to the fair, but George wouldn't ride in the bumper cars.

   _____

5. I saw the mystic she said that luck was on its way.

   _____

6. Paul wrote the check, he forgot to sign it.

   _____

7. She likes caramel ice cream, but chocolate is her favorite.

   _____

8. John started skateboarding, he's good at it.

   _____

9. Maria fed her leftover bread to the birds.

   _____

10. Wiley's is a bookstore local authors sometimes speak there.

    _____

◆D Check Up

For each item, circle the letter of the complete sentence.

1. A Sheetal is weaving a rug, it is red, green, and gold.

   B Nick takes the early train.

   C Phoebe's cat had four kittens, I hope I will get one of them.

   D Kay owns two big dogs she wants to move to the country.

2. F Kate and Brenna had dinner at home they made tacos.

   G Julia is enjoying Rome, she feels homesick.

   H Red is his favorite color, it makes him feel strong.

   J Melissa teaches high school.

3. A The uptown bus is crowded.

   B I went to the cafe, my friend had already left.

   C My dog has fleas, I am taking him to the vet today.

   D Nathan's stories are funny he is a good writer.

4. F It's a beautiful evening, I'm going to cook on the grill.

   G Jake's birthday is today his friends are celebrating.

   H The rain spoiled our picnic.

   J It is the color of cherries it's making me hungry.

Read the paragraph and look at the underlined sections. Choose the answer that is written correctly for each underlined section.

(5) The Boston Marathon is one of the world's best-known races. It takes place every April. <u>Runners begin the race in Hopkinton and finish in Boston, the course is over 26 miles long.</u> To compete in such a long
(6) race, runners must be in excellent condition. <u>Winners have run the race in just over two hours isn't that amazing?</u>

5. A Runners begin the race in Hopkinton and finish. In Boston the course is over 26 miles long.

   B Runners begin the race in Hopkinton and finish in Boston. The course is over 26 miles long.

   C Runners begin the race in Hopkinton and finish in Boston and the course is over 26 miles long.

   D Correct as it is

6. F Winners have run the race. In just over two hours isn't that amazing?

   G Winners have run the race in just over two hours, isn't that amazing?

   H Winners have run the race in just over two hours. Isn't that amazing?

   J Correct as it is

Sentence Combining:
Compound Subjects and Predicates

Your writing is stronger if you avoid repeating sentence
parts. For example, the following sentences use the same
predicate over and over. Only the subject changes.

    <u>Max</u> got on the bus. <u>Alice</u> got on the bus.

    <u>I</u> got on the bus.

The three sentences can be combined. Simply
join the three subjects in one compound subject.

    <u>Max</u>, <u>Alice</u>, and <u>I</u> got on the bus.

**Read each item. If the sentences can be combined by joining subjects, write
the new sentence. If the sentences don't need to be combined, write** *Correct.*

1. The sportswear must be inventoried. The shoes must be inventoried.

   _____

2. The company grew last year. Four new salespeople were hired.

   _____

3. Tulips bloom in the spring. Daffodils bloom in the spring.

   _____

4. The Halloween party was great. Everyone wore costumes.

   _____

5. My husband took dancing lessons. I took dancing lessons.

   _____

6. Diane interviewed for the job. Tina interviewed for the job.

   _____

Short sentences with the same subject can get boring. This is true even when different words name the subject.

> Joe's boss praised his work. His boss gave him a bonus.
> Soon she promoted him.

You can combine the sentences by joining the predicates in a compound predicate.

> Joe's boss praised his work, gave him a bonus,
> and soon promoted him.

Read each item. If the sentences can be combined by joining the two predicates in a compound predicate, write the new sentence. If the sentences don't need to be combined, write _Correct_.

1. Alice Jensen gets up early. Mrs. Jensen walks her dog before going to work.

   _____

2. Chris mowed the lawn. He pruned the shrubs.

   _____

3. The control panel has 20 switches. Some of the switches are red.

   _____

4. The snow covered the ground. It drifted against the houses.

   _____

5. Tara entered the contest. The first prize was a car.

   _____

6. Erin sat by the window. She waited for the rain to stop.

   _____

7. Hailey brushed her hair. She braided it carefully. Then she tied the braids with yellow ribbon.

   _____

C Apply

Read each pair of underlined sentences. Circle the letter of the sentence that correctly combines the two sentences.

1. <u>The foreman called a meeting.</u>
   <u>The foreman explained the new safety rules.</u>

   A   The foreman called a meeting and the new safety rules were explained.

   B   The foreman called a meeting and explained the new safety rules.

2. <u>Dan got lost during his trip.</u>
   <u>Dan had to ask for directions during his trip.</u>

   A   Dan got lost during his trip and Dan got directions.

   B   Dan got lost and had to ask for directions during his trip.

3. <u>Sally rides a bike to work.</u>
   <u>Charlie rides a bike to work.</u>

   A   Sally rides a bike to work and Charlie rides.

   B   Sally and Charlie ride bikes to work.

4. <u>The officer slowly opened the door.</u>
   <u>The officer looked inside.</u>

   A   The officer slowly opened the door and looked inside.

   B   The officer slowly opened the door and the officer inside.

5. <u>Connie worked in the sales department.</u>
   <u>Jorge worked in the sales department.</u>

   A   Connie worked and Jorge worked in the sales department.

   B   Connie and Jorge worked in the sales department.

6. <u>The project is difficult.</u>
   <u>The project will take a long time to complete.</u>

   A   The project is difficult and it will take a long time to complete it.

   B   The project is difficult and will take a long time to complete.

7. <u>My sister's cookies taste delicious.</u>
   <u>Her pies taste delicious.</u>

   A   My sister's cookies and pies taste delicious.

   B   My sister's cookies taste delicious and her pies.

◆D Check Up

Read each set of underlined sentences. Circle the letter of the sentence that correctly combines the underlined sentences.

1. Hamid dug a trench across the field.
   Hamid laid drain tile in the trench.

   A Hamid dug a trench and laid drain tile across the field.

   B Hamid dug a trench across the field and laid drain tile in it.

   C Hamid dug a trench and across the field he laid drain tile in it.

   D Correct as it is

2. The shortstop caught the ball.
   The shortstop threw the ball to first base.

   F The shortstop caught the ball and threw it to first base.

   G The shortstop caught it and threw to first base the ball.

   H The shortstop caught the ball to first base, and he threw the ball.

   J Correct as it is

3. The department store is having a sale on shoes.
   I hope I can find a pair of sandals in my size.

   A The department store is having a sale on sandals in my size.

   B The department store is having a shoe sale, and I hope I can find sandals.

   C The department store is having a sale and, I hope I can find a pair.

   D Correct as it is

4. Ms. Lopez ran across the street.
   Ms. Lopez tripped.
   She broke the heel off her left shoe.

   F Ms. Lopez ran and tripped across the street and broke the heel off her left shoe.

   G Ms. Lopez ran across the street and tripped off the heel of her left shoe.

   H Ms. Lopez ran across the street, tripped, and broke the heel off her left shoe.

   J Correct as it is

A Introduce

Sentence Combining: More Compound Sentence Parts

You have learned to combine sentences by forming compound subjects and compound predicates. You can also combine sentences by forming other compound parts. Here are some examples:

Sentence 1: <u>Charles sent out the</u> newsletter.

Sentence 2: <u>Charles sent out the</u> current price list.

Combined: <u>Charles sent out the</u> newsletter and current price list.

Sentence 1: <u>Lois sends her daughter to</u> piano <u>lessons</u>.

Sentence 2: <u>Lois sends her daughter to</u> ballet <u>lessons</u>.

Combined: <u>Lois sends her daughter to</u> piano and ballet <u>lessons</u>.

Read each item. Underline the words that appear in both sentences. Then combine the two sentences by forming a compound part.

1. The jackhammer is loud. The jackhammer is annoying.

   _____

2. Moyra can speak Spanish. Moyra can speak French.

   _____

3. Ian types letters on the computer. Ian types reports on the computer.

   _____

4. Mr. Green repairs washing machines. Mr. Green repairs dishwashers.

   _____

5. The diamonds in the necklace are beautiful. The diamonds in the necklace are rare.

   _____

6. The candy machine takes coins. The candy machine takes dollar bills.

   _____

B ▶ Practice

Read each pair of underlined sentences. Circle the letter of the sentence that correctly combines the two underlined sentences.

1. Carol lives in a large house.
   Carol lives in a new house.

   A Carol lives in a large, new house.

   B Carol lives in a large house and in a new house.

2. The company pays cash for old cars.
   The company pays cash for broken appliances.

   A The company pays cash for old cars and broken appliances.

   B The company pays cash for old cars and cash for broken appliances.

3. Ms. Rush bought a sofa for her apartment.
   Ms. Rush bought a coffee table for her apartment.

   A Ms. Rush bough a sofa for her apartment and a coffee table.

   B Ms. Rush bought a sofa and a coffee table for her apartment.

4. I need to return these books to the library today.
   I need to return these books to the library before 5 o'clock.

   A I need to return these books to the library today before 5 o'clock.

   B I need to return these books and today and before 5 o'clock.

5. My aunt gave me a card on my birthday.
   My aunt gave me a check on my birthday.

   A My aunt gave me a card and a check on my birthday.

   B My aunt gave me a card on my birthday and a birthday check.

6. Ed entered the sack race at the fair.
   Ed entered the pie-eating contest at the fair.

   A Ed entered the sack race at the fair and he entered the pie-eating contest.

   B Ed entered the sack race and the pie-eating contest at the fair.

C ▸ Apply

Read each set of sentences. Decide whether the final sentence in each set combines the underlined ones correctly. If it does, write *Correct*. If it does not, rewrite the combined sentence correctly.

1. <u>Dad, I would like to borrow twenty dollars.</u>
   <u>Dad, I would like to borrow the car.</u>

   Dad, I would like to borrow twenty dollars and the car.

   _____

2. <u>Remember to pack a raincoat.</u>
   <u>Remember to pack an umbrella.</u>

   Remember to pack a raincoat and pack an umbrella.

   _____

3. <u>Tom enjoys adventure stories.</u>
   <u>Tom enjoys science fiction stories.</u>

   Tom enjoys adventure and science fiction stories.

   _____

4. <u>The bush has broad leaves.</u>
   <u>The bush has red berries.</u>

   The bush has broad red leaves and berries.

   _____

5. <u>The customer ordered a cup of coffee.</u>
   <u>The customer ordered a ham sandwich.</u>

   The customer ordered a cup and a coffee and a sandwich.

   _____

6. <u>The judges chose Janene quickly.</u>
   <u>The judges chose Janene unanimously.</u>

   The judges chose Janene quickly and, in addition, they chose her unanimously.

   _____

D Check Up

Read each set of underlined sentences. Circle the letter of the sentence that correctly combines the underlined sentences.

1. Inez hiked up the hill.
   Inez hiked down the valley.

   A Inez hiked up and down the hill and valley.

   B Inez hiked up the hill and she hiked down the valley.

   C Inez hiked up the hill and down the valley.

   D Inez hiked the hill and valley.

2. The shortstop hit two singles in the game.
   The shortstop hit a home run in the game.

   F In the game, the shortstop hit two singles and he hit a home run.

   G The shortstop hit two singles and a home run in the game.

   H The shortstop hit two singles and home runs in the game.

   J In the game, the shortstop hit singles and home runs.

3. Sasha received her paycheck.
   Then Sasha went to the bank.
   Sasha deposited her check in her savings account at the bank.

   A After Sasha received her paycheck, she went to the bank and deposited the check in her savings account.

   B After Sasha went to the bank, she received her paycheck and deposited it at the bank in her savings account.

   C After Sasha received her paycheck, she deposited her check and her savings account at the bank.

   D After Sasha went to the bank, she deposited her check and her savings account at the bank.

4. Laura asked for a promotion.
   Laura asked for a pay raise.

   F Laura asked for a promotion, pay raise.

   G Laura asked for a promotion and a pay raise.

   H Laura asked for a promotion and she asked for a pay raise.

   J Laura asked for a promotion, then a pay raise.

Sentence Combining: Adding Modifiers

When you're writing, think about how you can add details about the persons, places, and things you're describing. These details, or **modifiers**, make your writing more interesting. For example, an **adjective**, like *smart*, can modify a noun, like *girl*. You can often combine sentences to add modifiers.

Here are examples of combining sentences to add modifiers:

Adding an adjective:

> **Sentence 1:** We watched a <u>movie</u> last night.
>
> **Sentence 2:** The <u>movie</u> was <u>funny</u>.
>
> **Combined:** We watched a funny movie last night.

Adding an adjective phrase:

> **Sentence 1:** These <u>videotapes</u> are overdue.
>
> **Sentence 2:** The <u>videotapes</u> are <u>from the library</u>.
>
> **Combined:** These videotapes from the library are overdue.

Read each pair of sentences. Underline the noun that is modified in the second sentence of each pair. Underline the same noun in the first sentence. Then combine the sentences.

1. A bird escaped from the zoo last night. The bird is rare.

   _____

2. During their vacation, the Spivaks climbed a mountain. The mountain is in Oregon.

   _____

3. A dog led her master across the street. The dog is trained.

   _____

4. This ice cream tastes like fudge. The ice cream is in the blue carton.

   _____

5. Heath owns a sailboat. His sailboat is at Lakeside Dock.

   _____

B ▶ Practice

When you combine sentences and move modifers, be sure to keep modifiers with the correct words. Place an adjective *before* the noun it modifies. Place an adjective phrase *after* the noun it modifies.

In the following example, notice how misplacing a modifier changes the meaning of the sentence.

> **Original sentences:**
> A girl swam next to the dolphin.
> The dolphin was large.
> The girl was small.

> **Incorrect placement:**
> A large girl swam next to the small dolphin.

> **Correct placement:**
> A small girl swam next to the large dolphin.

Read each set of sentences. Decide whether the final sentence correctly combines the two underlined sentences. Write *Correct* or *Incorrect* on the line.

1. The painting shows a garden.
   The garden is oval.

   The oval painting shows a garden.   _____

2. Clouds covered the sky today.
   The clouds were dark.

   Clouds covered the dark sky today.   _____

3. Mrs. Smith bought a carpet for her house.
   The house is new.

   Mrs. Smith bought a carpet for her new house.   _____

4. Music filled the room.
   The music was loud.

   Loud music filled the room.   _____

5. Chili was heaped in a large bowl.
   The chili was spicy.

   Chili was heaped in a large, spicy bowl.   _____

Apply

Read each pair of underlined sentences. Circle the letter of the sentence that correctly combines the two underlined sentences.

1. <u>Clare bought a dress at the sale.</u>
   <u>The dress was short.</u>

   A Clare bought a dress at the sale and it was short.

   B Clare bought a short dress at the sale.

2. <u>Those books are half-price.</u>
   <u>The books are from the bookstore.</u>

   A Those books from the bookstore are half-price.

   B Those books are from the half-price bookstore.

3. <u>The messenger balanced several packages.</u>
   <u>The packages were bulky.</u>

   A The bulky messenger balanced several packages.

   B The messenger balanced several bulky packages.

4. <u>Our team will play the game tonight.</u>
   <u>The game is very important.</u>

   A It's very important that our team will play the game tonight.

   B Our team will play the very important game tonight.

5. <u>Volunteers made a play area.</u>
   <u>The play area was for their children.</u>

   A Volunteers are for their children and they made a play area.

   B Volunteers made a play area for their children.

6. <u>Rabbits ate the beans growing in my garden.</u>
   <u>The rabbits were young.</u>

   A Young rabbits ate the beans growing in my garden.

   B Rabbits ate the young beans growing in my garden.

Read each set of underlined sentences. Circle the letter of the sentence that correctly combines the underlined sentences.

1. Sam tapped his foot in time to the music.
    The music was lively.

    A Lively Sam tapped his foot in time to the music.

    B Sam tapped his lively foot in time to the music.

    C Sam is lively and he tapped his foot in time to the music.

    D Sam tapped his foot in time to the lively music.

2. The wind caused waves to crash against the ship.
    The wind was strong.
    The waves were huge.

    F The wind caused strong waves to crash against the huge ship.

    G The strong wind caused huge waves to crash against the ship.

    H The wind caused waves to crash against the ship and they were strong and huge.

    J The wind that was strong caused waves that were huge to crash against the ship.

3. Malik studies whales in the Atlantic Ocean.
    The whales are endangered.

    A Malik studies endangered whales in the Atlantic Ocean.

    B Malik studies whales in the endangered Atlantic Ocean.

    C Malik studies whales in the Atlantic Ocean and they are endangered.

    D Endangered Malik studies whales in the Atlantic Ocean.

4. A wall surrounds the houses.
    The wall is stone.
    The houses are in the village.

    F A wall in the village surrounds the stone houses.

    G A stone wall in the village surrounds the houses.

    H A stone wall surrounds the houses in the village.

    J A wall surrounds the stone houses that are in the village.

Sentence Combining: More About Adding Modifiers

Adverbs and adverb phrases add information about *how, when, where,* and *why* an action happens. They may also modify adjectives and other adverbs. You can make a sentence more powerful by combining it with an adverb from another sentence about the same topic.

> **Adding an adverb:**
>
> **Sentence 1:** The runner cleared the hurdle.
>
> **Sentence 2:** He did so <u>easily</u>.
>
> **Combined:** The runner easily cleared the hurdle.

> **Adding an adverb phrase:**
>
> **Sentence 1:** Cass drove a bus filled with tourists.
>
> **Sentence 2:** She took them <u>to the Capitol</u>.
>
> **Combined:** Cass drove a bus filled with tourists to the Capitol.

Each sentence in Column B is a combination of one of the sentence pairs in Column A. Write the letter of the Column B sentence on the line next to its Column A pair.

Column A

1. _____ The band leader waved his baton. He moved it in a steady rhythm.

2. _____ Brown bears searched for food. They looked at our campsite.

3. _____ Joe's ferry carries people and supplies. It goes to South Bass Island.

4. _____ Clare smiled at the good news. She smiled happily.

5. _____ Our dog had puppies. She gave birth yesterday.

Column B

A Brown bears searched for food at our campsite.

B Clare smiled happily at the good news.

C The band leader waved his baton in a steady rhythm.

D Yesterday our dog had puppies.

E Joe's ferry carries people and supplies to South Bass Island.

B ▶ Practice

Combine each pair of sentences. Be sure to place the adverb or adverb phrase from the second sentence correctly.

1. The pilot made an emergency announcement.
   He spoke calmly.

   _____

2. Two lions crept to the water hole.
   They moved silently.

   _____

3. Flu spread through the office.
   It happened slowly.

   _____

4. Al swam in the river.
   He went against the current.

   _____

5. Dan and Carole hiked for two hours.
   They hiked every night.

   _____

6. Taylor applied for the job.
   She did so eagerly.

   _____

7. We painted the house for three hours.
   We worked before the rain began.

   _____

8. The boat rocked in the choppy water.
   It moved back and forth.

   _____

 **Apply**

Read each set of sentences. Decide whether the final sentence combines the underlined ones correctly. If it does, write *Correct*. If it does not, rewrite the combined sentence correctly.

1. My son spoke at his commencement.
   He spoke proudly.
   He spoke clearly.

   My son spoke at his commencement, proudly and clearly, too.

   _____

2. Jim entered the county fair.
   He went through the main gate.

   Jim entered the county fair, and he went through the main gate.

   _____

3. Thick mud covered the dog's feet.
   They were covered completely.

   Thick mud completely covered the dog's feet.

   _____

4. The band played "Stars and Stripes Forever."
   They played on the Fourth of July.

   The band played on the Fourth of July and it was "Stars and Stripes Forever."

   _____

5. The fire spread through the dry woods.
   The fire spread quickly.
   It spread uncontrollably.

   The fire spread quickly and uncontrollably through the dry woods.

   _____

D Check Up

Read each set of underlined sentences. Circle the letter of the sentence that correctly combines the underlined sentences.

1. Lee steered his wheelchair through the crowd.
   He moved expertly.

   A Lee steered his wheelchair and moved expertly through the crowd.

   B Lee expertly steered his wheelchair through the crowd.

   C Lee steered his wheelchair through the crowd, and he did so expertly.

   D Lee, who moved expertly, steered his wheelchair through the crowd.

2. Fireflies darted in the garden.
   They darted swiftly.
   They darted among the flowers.

   F Fireflies darted swiftly, and they darted in the garden among the flowers.

   G Fireflies darted among the flowers swiftly in the garden.

   H Fireflies darted swiftly among the flowers in the garden.

   J Fireflies darted among the flowers and swiftly in the garden.

3. Water seeped out of the old pipe.
   It came out slowly.

   A Water seeped out of the old pipe in a slowly way.

   B Water seeped out of the old pipe, and it came out slowly.

   C Slowly water seeped, and it came out of the old pipe.

   D Water slowly seeped out of the old pipe.

4. Mel tossed the tickets into the trash.
   He threw them carelessly.

   F Careless Mel tossed the tickets into the trash.

   G In a careless way, Mel tossed the tickets into the trash.

   H Mel carelessly tossed the tickets into the trash.

   J Mel tossed the tickets into the trash, and he threw them carelessly.

Complete Sentences and Fragments

A complete sentence has both a subject and a predicate. The subject names the person or thing acting. The predicate tells what the subject does and always includes a verb.

> Voters in this election | will choose the city's leaders.
>   subject   predicate (The verb is underlined.)

A fragment lacks one or both of these parts. To correct a fragment, provide the missing part or parts.

Run-On Sentences

A run-on sentence combines two or more sentences with no punctuation or with only a comma between the sentences. To correct a run-on sentence, provide the correct end mark at the end of the first sentence, and begin the second sentence with a capital letter.

> **Run-on:**   The radio was much too loud, it hurt our ears.

> **Corrected:** The radio was much too loud! It hurt our ears.

Sentence Combining: Compound Parts

A short passage in which phrases or sentence parts are repeated is weak. To strengthen such writing, combine the sentences by forming compound sentence parts.

> **Repeated predicate:** Monday was cold. Tuesday was cold.
> **Compound subject:** Monday and Tuesday were cold.
>
> **All parts repeated except modifier:** Jason read a short poem. He read a
>   funny poem.
>
> **Compound modifier:** Jason read a short and funny poem.

Sentence Combining: Adding Modifiers

Writing is weak if details about a single topic are spread over several short sentences. To strengthen such writing, combine the sentences by moving modifiers from the weaker sentence(s) to the strongest sentence.

> **Scattered details:** The umpire threw out the player. The player was
>   shouting. The umpire acted immediately.

> **Modifiers added:** The umpire immediately threw out the shouting player.

Choose the sentence that is written correctly. Be sure the sentence you choose is not a run-on or a fragment.

1. A No later than three o'clock in the afternoon.

   B One vase holds red roses, there are at least five blooms.

   C Ran for the train but missed it.

   D Everybody kept the secret.

2. F The coupon is worth a dollar.

   G Because the pipe under the sink was clogged.

   H Misty had cereal Joel had toast.

   J All sorts of cottages with gardens around them.

3. A On the right hand side of the photograph of the train.

   B What happened, I wasn't paying attention.

   C Who knows the answer to the riddle?

   D A low rumble like thunder.

4. F Wants a clown at her daughter's first birthday party.

   G The artist painted birds and flowers.

   H The plastic chairs on the patio.

   J The electric clocks show the wrong time, we lost power during the night.

Read the passage and look at the underlined parts. Choose the answers below that are written correctly for each underlined part.

(5) <u>My brother's house looked shabby. Needed a new coat of paint.</u> Pete wanted to have the job done by a pro. He asked everyone he knew

(6) for suggestions. <u>One woman on his street gave Pete the name of a good painter, Pete hired him.</u> Now Pete's house looks as good as new.

5. A My brother's house looked shabby. He needed a new coat of paint.

   B My brother's house looked shabby. It needed a new coat of paint.

   C My brother's house looked shabby needed a new coat of paint.

   D Correct as it is

6. F One woman on his street gave Pete the name of a good painter. Pete hired him.

   G One woman on his street gave Pete the name of a good painter Pete hired him.

   H One woman on his street. Gave Pete the name of a good painter. Pete hired him.

   J Correct as it is

Read each set of underlined sentences. Circle the letter of the sentence that correctly combines the underlined sentences.

7. Jennifer took the clean clothes from the dryer.
She sorted the clean clothes.
She put the clothes away.

   A Jennifer took the clean clothes, sorted them, and put the clothes away from the dryer.

   B Jennifer took and sorted and put the clean clothes away from the dryer.

   C After Jennifer took the clean clothes from the dryer and before she put the dryer away, she sorted the clothes.

   D Jennifer took the clean clothes from the dryer, sorted them, and put them away.

8. The high school band marched in the town's Memorial Day parade.
The Boy Scouts marched in the parade.

   F The high school band and the Boy Scouts marched in the town's Memorial Day Parade.

   G The high school band marched, and the Boy Scouts marched, too, in the town's Memorial Day Parade.

   H The high school band marched to the Boy Scouts in the town's Memorial Day Parade.

   J The only groups who marched in the town's Memorial Day Parade were the high school band and the Boy Scouts.

9. A messenger came to the office late in the day.
He dropped off three packages.

   A A messenger came to the office and dropped off three packages that were late.

   B A messenger came to the office late in the day and dropped off three packages.

   C A messenger came and dropped off three packages to the office later.

   D A messenger came to the office to drop off packages, and there were three, and he came late in the day.

10. The two children waved to the lifeguard.
    The children were in the pool.
    The pool was huge.

    A The two children waved to the lifeguard in the pool, which was huge.

    B The two children in the huge pool waved to the lifeguard.

    C The two children in the pool, which was huge, waved to the lifeguard.

    D The two children who were in the pool waved to the lifeguard, and the pool was huge.

11. Shoppers crowded into the shoe department.
    Many shoppers came.
    They pressed in eagerly.

    F Many shoppers crowded eagerly into the shoe department.

    G Many shoppers crowded into the shoe department, where they were eagerly pressed in.

    H Shoppers crowded into the shoe department, and many pressed in eagerly.

    J A crowd of shoppers pressed in eagerly into the shoe department.

12. Audrey answered the phone.
    She spoke sleepily.
    The phone was her cell phone.

    A When Audrey answered her cell phone, she was sleepy.

    B The phone Audrey answered when she spoke sleepily was a cell phone.

    C Audrey answered the phone and spoke sleepily into her cell phone.

    D Audrey sleepily answered her cell phone.

13. Be sure to take a flashlight on the hike.
    The hike will be a night hike.
    The flashlight should be reliable.

    F Be sure to take a flashlight when you hike at night, and it should be reliable.

    G Be sure to take a flashlight that is reliable on the night hike.

    H Be sure to take a reliable flashlight on the night hike.

    J Be sure that any flashlight you take on a night hike is reliable.

A ▶ Introduce

The Topic Sentence of a Paragraph

A paragraph is a group of sentences that work together to tell about a single idea. The most important idea of a paragraph is called its **main idea**. The **topic sentence** of a paragraph states the main idea.

Not every paragraph has a topic sentence. Even without one, readers can figure out the paragraph's main idea. But a topic sentence is useful to both readers and writers. It lets readers know what to focus on. It helps writers keep to their topic.

Read the following paragraph. Its topic sentence is underlined. The topic sentence lets readers know that the paragraph will be about the many uses of mustard. The writer has been guided by the topic sentence. He or she has included only examples of how mustard is used.

> <u>Over the years, people have found many uses for mustard.</u> Prepared mustard is, of course, a good way to add flavor to dull foods. Mixed with water, mustard powder may cure hiccups. Or it may make a sore elbow feel better. Sprinkled in your shoes, it may protect you from frostbite.

Read each paragraph. Then circle the letter beside its topic sentence.

1. Fireflies don't do any harm. Unlike some bugs, they don't carry disease. They don't bite like mosquitoes, nor do they sting like bees. Fireflies don't even fly very fast. That means they make no unpleasant noise.

    A Unlike some bugs, they don't carry disease.

    B Fireflies don't do any harm.

    C Fireflies don't even fly very fast.

2. The cheetah is the fastest land animal in the world. It can run faster than a cougar or a puma. It can even beat a racehorse. At top speed, the cheetah can run up to 70 mph. That's faster than most cars on the highway.

    F At top speed, the cheetah can run up to 70 mph.

    G The cheetah is the fastest land animal in the world.

    H It can run faster than a cougar or a puma.

B Practice

Read each paragraph below. Then choose its topic sentence from among the four lettered sentences. Write the letter of the topic sentence on the line.

A Emus are unusual and playful birds.

B Bebe Chalker has lived all over the world.

C Doll clothes have changed to reflect the times.

D Clara Barton was one of America's greatest heroines.

E Elephants in the wild need a lot of water.

1. _____ She cared for troops during the Civil War. After the war, she was in charge of a search for missing soldiers. For years she fought for the rights of freed slaves. Of course, she is best known for founding the American Red Cross and serving as its first president.

2. _____ Unlike most other birds, they cannot fly. The males, not the females, sit on the eggs until they hatch. These large birds like to run and swim in groups. Sometimes they hop up and down like pogo sticks. They have even been known to get on the ground and roll over like dogs.

3. _____ She was born in the African country of Nigeria. When she was two years old, her family moved to Singapore, in Asia. She went to boarding school in England. Then she went to college in the United States. Bebe now lives in Lima, Peru.

4. _____ They can drink up to forty gallons of water at a time. They also like to bathe every day. If the water is deep enough, they will lie down in it. If not, they can use their trunks to give themselves a shower.

5. _____ In the past, female dolls used to come only with dresses and ribbons. In those days, no one expected girls to want careers. But times have changed. Now female dolls come with work suits and briefcases. Some of them even come with overalls and toolboxes.

◆C Apply

Write a topic sentence for each of the following paragraphs.

1. _____. Elvis has sold over one billion records. That is more than any other artist. He won many of music's top awards. People from all over the world visit his house, Graceland. Elvis died in 1977. But his music and his fame live on.

   _____

   _____

2. _____. They have similar lifespans and mating habits. Like the jaguar, the puma is very large and very strong. Both jaguars and pumas prey on deer. They both live mainly in Central and South America.

   _____

   _____

3. _____. We all know the common tomato. But tomatoes also come in green and yellow. They come in different sizes, too. One small kind of tomato is the plum tomato. An even smaller kind is the cherry tomato. No matter how they look, tomatoes taste delicious.

   _____

   _____

4. _____. Eggs can be scrambled or fried. They can be hard-boiled or soft-boiled. Some people order their eggs over-easy or over-medium. Some like their eggs poached or deviled. Some athletes even drink eggs raw out of a glass!

   _____

   _____

Read each paragraph below. Then circle the letter of its topic sentence.

1. _____ First, large drawings are tacked onto the walls of the palace. Then thousands of ears of corn are chosen for their colors. Each ear is sliced lengthwise. Finally, workers carefully nail the ears into place.

   A Corn is a tasty food.

   B Decorating the Corn Palace is a hard job.

   C The Corn Palace is in South Dakota.

   D Corn is grown all over America.

2. _____ You can order them with syrup, jam, or honey. You can get them with blueberries or bananas. You can even have waffles instead of bread for your sandwich!

   F At Lulu's you can have waffles any way you want.

   G Lulu's opened in 1980.

   H Waffles can be round or square.

   J Lulu eats half a grapefruit every morning.

3. _____ One of the biggest differences is that whales need to breathe air, while fish do not. Another difference is that fish lay eggs, while whales give birth to live babies. And of course, most whales are much bigger than fish.

   A Whales are very different from fish.

   B Water in the ocean is salty.

   C Whales eat fish.

   D Moby Dick is a famous whale.

4. _____ It is a common food all over the world. A few grains of rice in a salt shaker will keep the salt from getting clumpy. Rice can be thrown at a newly married couple for good luck.

   F Rice and potatoes are both starches.

   G Rice has many uses.

   H It takes about half an hour to cook rice.

   J Rice tastes good with soy sauce.

Finding the Topic Sentence

A paragraph may include a **topic sentence** that states its main idea. Often the topic sentence is the first sentence of the paragraph. It leads readers into the paragraph. They can check back to the topic sentence. They can see how each detail fits with the main idea. Here is an example:

> <u>Seattle is a beautiful city</u>. It is surrounded by water. To its west is Puget Sound. A large lake lies to the east. On a clear day, residents can see snow-capped mountains in the distance. The city also has many pretty parks to enjoy.

Sometimes the topic sentence is in another place in a paragraph. Whether it is in the middle or at the end, it can summarize what has come before. It can restate what the writer has said. Here is an example:

> If you visit San Francisco, you can go to art museums. You can see plays. You can dance yourself silly in one of the city's nightclubs. You can sip wine that comes straight from nearby vineyards. You can get around by riding cable cars up and down the hilly streets. <u>There are many ways to have fun in San Francisco.</u>

Underline the topic sentence in each of the following paragraphs.

1. There are two main kinds of coffee: arabica and robusta. About 70 percent of the world's coffee is arabica. This kind of coffee is mild. Robusta, on the other hand, is a more bitter coffee. It is also higher in caffeine.

2. The northern parts of Mexico have much desert land. Other parts of the country are lush and wet. There are even jungles in the far south. Some areas of Mexico can get very hot. But snow can be seen year-round on the tops of the great volcanoes. Mexico is a land of diverse climates.

3. Windsurfing has become a popular sport all over the world. Some people try it for the first time while on vacation. Many fall in love with it. There are now over a million windsurfers in Europe alone. It has even been made a new Olympic sport.

B Practice

Read each paragraph below. Then circle the letter beside its topic sentence.

1. Cave drawings teach us much about early humans. They show us what kinds of animals they hunted. Through them we learn about the tools that cave dwellers used. The drawings also give us glimpses into early humans' home lives. Finally, they show us that art has always been a part of human life.

    A They show us what kinds of animals they hunted.

    B Cave drawings teach us much about early humans.

    C Through them we learn about the tools that cave dwellers used.

    D Finally, they show us that art has always been a part of human life.

2. You can buy King Cakes in most stores during Mardi Gras in New Orleans. The colorful cake has a small plastic baby doll hidden inside it. The person who finds the baby doll in his or her piece is crowned "king." The only real duty of the king is to buy the next cake. The King Cake is a great Mardi Gras tradition.

    F The King Cake is a great Mardi Gras tradition.

    G The only real duty of the king is to buy the next cake.

    H You can buy King Cakes in most stores during Mardi Gras in New Orleans.

    J The colorful cake has a small plastic baby doll hidden inside it.

3. Long ago, the Stone of Destiny was a Scottish treasure. It was the seat on which Scottish kings and queens were crowned. In 1297 the stone was stolen by the king of England. For many years, the English kept the stone on display in London. Recently, England decided that it should be returned to Scotland. But now people can't agree on which city it should go to. And is it the real stone? Some believe that the stone in London is a fake. They say the real stone is hidden. All in all, the Stone of Destiny has had a long and troubled history.

    A For many years, the English kept the stone on display in London.

    B In 1297 the stone was stolen by the king of England.

    C Some believe that the stone in London is a fake.

    D All in all, the Stone of Destiny has had a long and troubled history.

The topic sentence is missing in each of the following paragraphs. On the lines below each paragraph, write a topic sentence for the paragraph.

1. _____. They eat anything and everything. That includes gophers, grass, insects, roots, and berries. They can eat 80 pounds of fish per day. It may seem greedy, but there is a good reason. Bears need to store up a lot of fat to live through the long winter.

   _____

   _____

2. _____. Maroon shell fireworks simply make a loud bang. Ring shells explode in a ring of stars. Willow fireworks also explode into stars. But these stars fall toward the ground in the shape of willow branches. Be thankful there are so many kinds. Each one brings out a different "ooh" or "aah."

   _____

   _____

3. When elephants look for food, they make rumbling noises in their throats. If an elephant senses danger, it goes quiet. The silence puts the other elephants on alert. Another signal is the trumpeting noise. This noise does two things. It warns friends and scares away enemies. _____.

   _____

   _____

4. _____. An oral surgeon removes teeth. An endodontist works on the nerves that connect to the teeth. A periodontist cares for the gums. An orthodontist installs braces to straighten teeth. Of course, we'd all prefer not to visit any of them!

   _____

   _____

Each paragraph below is missing a topic sentence. Read each paragraph. Then decide which of the choices would be a correct topic sentence.

1. _____. Tortillas, found at most Mexican meals, are made from ground maize. Legend has it that an Aztec god turned himself into an ant. Then he stole one grain of maize from inside a mountain. He gave this grain to humans to feed them for all times.

   A Maize has always been an important food in Mexico.

   B Ants always spoil a picnic.

   C An ant can easily get inside a mountain.

   D Maize is especially delicious when ground and cooked with butter.

2. _____. There were miners and gamblers. There were writers and millionaires. A dancer named Lola Montez walked around with a whip. Every now and then, she cracked the whip in the air. An odd man named Oofty Goofty dressed himself in fur and feathers. He charged people a dime to kick him.

   F Mining for gold can be dangerous.

   G The Gold Rush took place in the late 1800s.

   H San Francisco is a center of business.

   J During the Gold Rush, San Francisco was full of odd characters.

3. Orange juice is a well-known source of Vitamin C. Other liquid sources include grapefruit juice, tomato juice, and the juices of various berries. Vitamin C can actually be found in most fruits and vegetables. Even potato skins have Vitamin C. _____.

   A Vitamin C is better than Vitamin B.

   B Oranges have more Vitamin C than strawberries have.

   C It is easy to get your daily dose of Vitamin C.

   D You should eat potato skins with every meal.

A Introduce

Developing Paragraphs with Details and Examples

Every sentence in a paragraph should be related to the main idea. The **topic sentence** often introduces readers to the main idea. The other sentences are called **supporting sentences.** They give more information about the main idea.

In paragraphs that describe something, supporting sentences often give **sensory details.** These details tell how a thing looks, sounds, smells, feels, or tastes. Here is an example:

> It was a perfect day for football. The cloudless sky was bright blue. The air was crisp and cool with just a hint of winter. The smell of dried leaves floated in the air. Apple cider from the snack stand tasted sweet and tangy. The sound of the school band echoed across the stadium.

In other paragraphs, the supporting sentences give **examples**.

> Some people say that the number 13 is unlucky. But it has always been my lucky number. I was born on November 13. I met my husband on October 13, and we married on June 13. We live happily at 1300 Oak Street. I even won the lottery playing 1313. Say what you like about 13, but I love that number.

One sentence in each paragraph below is underlined. Is it the topic sentence or a supporting sentence? Write *Topic Sentence* or *Supporting Sentence* on the line.

1. There is plenty to do in Atlantic City. <u>You can stroll along the world's first boardwalk.</u> You can eat funnel cakes. You can stay in a hotel shaped like an elephant. And, of course, you can try your luck in the famous casinos.

    _____

2. <u>The heat last Monday was unbearable.</u> All day long the sun was scorching. The city plaza felt like a giant sauna. People were drenched in sweat. Even the children were complaining.

    _____

Read each paragraph below. Decide whether the supporting sentences develop the paragraph using sensory details or examples. Write *Sensory Details* or *Examples* on the line.

1.   People on vegan diets eat no animal products. This rules out more foods than you would think. For example, vegans don't have butter or cream cheese on their bagels. They don't have pasta either. After all, noodles are made with eggs. Most cookie recipes call for eggs or milk. For that reason, cookies may be on the list of forbidden foods.

_____

2.   Cindy had cleaned the house from top to bottom. It looked beautiful. The windows squeaked when she touched them. The tiles in the bathroom gleamed. The wooden furniture was polished to a shine. A springtime lemon smell filled every room.

_____

3.   Charlottesville, Virginia, is proud to have been Thomas Jefferson's home. Several streets in town bear the former president's name. Statues of Jefferson have been put up all over town. Residents always bring their guests to see Jefferson's house, Monticello.

_____

4.   My neighbor, Henry, can fix anything. He has two antique cars that run like new. When my washer broke, I called Henry. Within an hour, he had it working better than ever. Last week, Henry was in an office building. His elevator got stuck between floors. Henry took out his Swiss army knife and pried open a panel. Soon the elevator was moving again.

_____

5.   Joe and Elena had a romantic dinner at Zin. Warm candlelight flickered on their table. Soft guitar music floated through the room. The waiter uncorked their wine bottle with a soft pop. The wine tasted smooth and rich on their tongues. The food was spicy and perfect for sharing.

_____

C ◆ Apply

Read each paragraph. On the lines, write one more supporting sentence for each paragraph. Follow the directions in parentheses.

1.   The kids left the house an absolute mess. Oily peanut butter was streaked across the wall. Potato chip crumbs were ground into the carpet. The smell of spoiled milk filled the kitchen. _____. (Add a sentence with a sensory detail.)

_____

_____

2.   Mr. Roberts is a bad supervisor. He comes to work half an hour late and leaves half an hour early. He supervises eighteen people but knows the names of only five of them. He is almost always rude. _____. (Add a sentence with an example.)

_____

_____

3.   It was a perfect day at the beach. The sun shone brightly. The air was warm and smelled salty. You could hear the waves lapping the shore. _____. (Add a sentence with a sensory detail.)

_____

_____

4.   Everyone I know uses home remedies. My brother wears catnip oil to keep away bugs. My boss washes her hair in beer to keep it shiny. My mother swallows raw garlic when she feels a cold coming on. _____. (Add a sentence with an example.)

_____

_____

D ► Check Up

Read each topic sentence. Then choose the answer that best develops the topic sentence.

1. Cats and dogs are different in many ways.

    A Cats spend a lot of time cleaning themselves. They sleep lightly.

    B Cats are often scared of dogs. Don't put a dog in the same room with a frightened cat.

    C Grown cats should not drink milk. It is bad for their stomachs.

    D Cats like to be by themselves for much of the day. Dogs are happiest when they are with their owners.

2. Lee and Maggie's wedding day didn't turn out as they'd planned.

    F Maggie's parents have a great marriage. They've been together for thirty years.

    G They first met in a coffee shop. Maggie asked to read part of Lee's newspaper.

    H The weather forecast had said it would be sunny. But it rained all day long.

    J A bride wears something old, something new, something borrowed, and something blue.

3. Knowing how to play the piano can come in handy.

    A You have to practice scales over and over again. It can take months to learn a simple tune.

    B At times, groups need someone to play "The Star-Spangled Banner." And "Happy Birthday" sounds even better when sung with a piano.

    C "Chopsticks" is a song that many people can play on the piano. It may be the easiest song to learn.

    D The flute is better than the piano. It is portable. You can take a flute anywhere.

A Introduce

Developing Paragraphs with Facts, Figures, and Reasons

Some paragraphs support the topic sentence using **facts and figures**. Here is an example:

> Whales can hold their breath for a long time. Usually, baleen whales breathe every 5 to 15 minutes. But they have been known to make a breath last as long as 40 minutes. The sperm whale may take a breath only once every 75 minutes.

To develop other paragraphs, writers use **reasons** to support their topic sentences. Here is an example:

> Many people were surprised when Allen Black was elected. He had been running behind in all the polls. His opponents outspent him. None of the newspapers had backed him. Even his own manager seemed discouraged on the day before the election.

One sentence in each paragraph below is underlined. Is it the topic sentence or a supporting sentence? Write *Topic Sentence* or *Supporting Sentence* on the line.

1. Roaches can live for one week without any water. They can live for four to five weeks without food. Amazingly, a roach can even live up to seven days after its head has been cut off. <u>Roaches are true survivors.</u>

   _____

2. Trina and Ty make a perfect couple. <u>Trina loves music, and Ty plays in a jazz band.</u> Ty loves dogs. Trina has two collies and a cocker spaniel. Both Trina and Ty love dancing and cooking. They even have the same favorite sandwich: a Reuben with extra mustard.

   _____

B ◆ Practice

Read each paragraph below. Decide how the supporting sentences develop the paragraph. Write *Facts and Figures* or *Reasons* on the line.

1.   A seatbelt could save your life in a car crash. Experts say that seatbelts save 9,500 lives in the United States alone each year. They reduce the risk of being killed in a crash by 45 percent. The message is getting out to Americans. In the early 1980s, only 12 percent of drivers used them. Now that figure has climbed to 69 percent.

      _____

2.   Providence, Rhode Island, is a good place to live. Housing is cheaper there than in nearby Boston or New York. The city has its own lively arts scene. It boasts many great restaurants. For summer fun, a short drive can take you from Providence to some great beaches.

      _____

3.   Racing pigeons can find their way home against the odds. One pigeon was released in Central Africa. It flew home to England. The journey took 55 days. The pigeon had to fly over 7,000 miles. In a famous study, 100 pigeons were released in Nevada. A whopping 98 found their way back home to New York.

      _____

4.   Carmen has decided to go to the nearby state college. The small size of the school is right for her. Also, the college offers good aid packages. The school's business department is strong. And she will be close to her family.

      _____

5.   Women are more likely than men to have headaches. One report shows that women have 85 percent more migraines than men. They have 59 percent more tension headaches. And 20 percent of women have headaches related to their monthly cycles.

      _____

Read each paragraph. On the lines, write one more supporting sentence for the paragraph. Follow the directions in parentheses.

1.   You might be getting a lot of caffeine even if you don't drink coffee. A can of Coke has 45.6 mg of caffeine. That's about half the amount that's in a cup of coffee. A can of Mountain Dew has 55 mg. _____. (Add a sentence with a fact or a figure. You can make up the fact or figure if you need to.)

_____

_____

2.   The newest action movie is not worth seeing. The gunfights are boring. The plot is not believable at all. The supposed bad guy is no scarier than a teddy bear. _____. (Add a sentence with a reason.)

_____

_____

3.   The Statue of Liberty is no little lady. She weighs 45,000 pounds. She is 152 feet tall. One hand is 16 feet, 5 inches long. A single fingernail is 13 inches by 10 inches. _____. (Add a sentence with a fact or a figure. You can make up the fact or figure if you need to.)

_____

_____

4.   Of all the holidays, the Fourth of July is the most fun. Family and friends gather together. You go swimming or play outdoor sports. Then you have a big cookout with all of your favorite foods. _____. (Add a sentence with a reason.)

_____

_____

D Check Up

Read each topic sentence. Then choose the answer that best develops the topic sentence.

1. Moving to Hawaii was a bad choice for Bella.

   A Hawaii is made up of seven different islands. The largest island is Oahu.

   B She's never liked swimming or going to the beach. She prefers sledding and ice skating.

   C She is 5 feet, 6 inches tall. She has black hair and dark brown eyes.

   D Bella loves everything about Hawaii. She goes hiking and scuba diving every weekend.

2. If you are ever arrested, you should know your rights.

   F You can be pulled over for driving over the speed limit. On most highways, the speed limit is 65 miles per hour.

   G They caught the man who robbed Miller's store. He was arrested coming out of a gas station.

   H Driving is a privilege. It is not a right. This privilege can be taken away from you.

   J You have the right to have a lawyer. You don't have to answer any questions before your lawyer arrives.

3. Claws are important to cats.

   A If you are clawed by a cat, you should get medical treatment. Wash the scratch with alcohol.

   B Cats are among the most graceful creatures on Earth. They always land on their feet.

   C Claws help a cat to climb. They are also important for hunting and defense.

   D Removing a cat's claws is now against some countries' laws. In past ages, however, cats were not treated well.

Recognizing Sequence Using Key Words

Many paragraphs present details in **time order,** or chronological sequence. Often, writers use key words to show time order. Some of those key words are *first, second, next, then, last,* and *finally.* When you read, watch for key words. When you write, use key words to help readers follow what is happening.

In this paragraph, events in a story are listed in time order.

> Sonya had a good time shopping at the mall. *First*, she stopped at the department store to buy a dress. *Then* she visited the shoe store. *Finally*, she bought herself an ice cream sundae at the candy store.

In this paragraph, steps in a process are listed in time order.

> Glass blowing is a painstaking art. *First*, glass is heated until it becomes liquid. *Next,* a worker dips a hollow iron pipe into the liquid glass. The worker *then* blows into the pipe. A glass balloon comes out of the other end of the pipe. *After that*, the worker can shape the glass. *Finally*, the shaped glass is broken away from the pipe.

Read the following paragraph. Then choose the correct answer to each question.

> Sailor Joseph Lee was on the crew of a cargo ship that sank in the South Pacific. Splashing about in the wreckage all alone, Lee found the escape raft and climbed aboard. At first, he lived on one jug of fresh water and some dry biscuits. Then the biscuits ran out. After that, Lee made a fishing hook out of a bent nail and some string. He began to catch fish. Soon after, the fresh-water jug ran dry. Clever Lee strung up some cloth to collect dew and rainwater. He survived at sea for 98 days until he reached land.

1. What happened after the biscuits ran out?

   A Lee found the escape raft and climbed aboard.

   B Lee's ship sank in the South Pacific.

   C Lee made a fishing hook out of a bent nail and some string.

2. What happened right before Lee strung up the cloth?

   F The cargo ship sank in the South Pacific.

   G The fresh-water jug ran dry.

   H Lee found the escape raft and climbed aboard.

B ▶ Practice

Read each paragraph. Then write five sentences for each paragraph describing its events in time order. Each sentence should tell about one event.

According to a Kwakiutl (Native American) creation myth, a raven flying over water could find nowhere to land. He decided to create a world. First, he dropped small pebbles to make islands. Second, he created trees and grass. Next, he made beasts to live in the forests. Then he made birds fly in the air above and fish swim in the sea below. Finally, he created man and woman out of clay and wood. This made the world complete.

1. _____

2. _____

3. _____

4. _____

5. _____

The students at Moore Middle School raised over $8,000 for victims of a hurricane. First, they held a bake sale and a car wash. Next, they used the proceeds to buy some old pieces of furniture. Then they refinished the pieces. After that, the students were able to sell the furniture at high prices. Finally, they sent all the money they had made to the hurricane relief fund.

6. _____

7. _____

8. _____

9. _____

10. _____

Read each topic sentence. Then read the four sentences below it. These sentences are out of order. Beside the first event in time order, write *First*. Beside the second event, write *Second*. Beside the third, write *Third*. Beside the last event, write *Finally*.

1. Frogs go through three stages before they become adults.

   _____, they are tiny eggs laid in the water.

   _____, the tadpole gets bigger and grows legs and the body of a frog.

   _____, the eggs hatch, and the frogs become legless tadpoles.

   _____, the frog becomes an adult.

2. Roping a calf is a skill learned by all cowboys.

   _____, the cowboy makes a large loop at the end of his rope.

   _____, with the calf securely roped, he ties the other end of the rope to his saddlehorn.

   _____, he flings the loop around the calf's head.

   _____, whirling the loop, he rides up next to the calf.

3. One of the most famous hibernators is the sleepy dormouse.

   _____, it falls asleep, with its heart slowing down to one beat every few minutes.

   _____, it stores up lots of body fat all through the autumn.

   _____, it wakes up restored from its long rest.

   _____, as winter comes on, it builds a nest in the tree roots.

4. The glass in windows is made using a special process.

   _____, the molten glass is poured onto a pool of molten tin.

   _____, the molten glass spreads out, cools, and hardens.

   _____, soda ash, limestone, and sand are put into a furnace.

   _____, the hot furnace melts the ingredients into molten glass.

◆D Check Up

In each paragraph, details are presented in time order. However, one sentence is missing. Read each paragraph. Then circle the letter of the sentence that belongs on the line.

1.   The movie detective described the events to the roomful of suspects. _____. He went up to the first floor. There, he was surprised by the rich man, who found him stealing rare books from his study. A fight began. The thief grabbed his flashlight. He struck the rich man and ran out of the room. Finally, he left the house.

   A The rich man's blood was on the thief's flashlight.

   B The thief and the rich man were longtime rivals.

   C First, the thief threw the flashlight into the bushes.

   D First, the thief entered the house through the basement window.

2.   The actress who plays Time Cat works on her make-up for two hours every night. First, she paints her arms, legs, and neck with black and white stripes. Second, she smears a base of white greasepaint all over her face. Next, she paints the numbers and hands of a clock on her face.

      _____.

   F Next, she practices her meowing.

   G Finally, she puts on a cat-nose, whiskers, and pointy ears.

   H Finally, she takes all of the make-up off.

   J In her last play, she dressed as a Greek goddess.

3.   John, Jeff, and Jett went all-out preparing for their Super Bowl party. _____. Next, they decorated the living room with banners. After that, they filled ten bowls with snacks. Then they filled coolers with soft drinks. Finally, they opened the door for their guests.

   A At halftime, they swept the kitchen.

   B First, they ate enough pizza to feed a small village.

   C They were sad because the Bears weren't in the Super Bowl.

   D First, they cleaned the house from top to bottom.

Recognizing Sequence Without Using Key Words

Sometimes writers do not use key words to make time order clear. In these cases, readers must pay close attention to each sentence. They should picture events as they happen.

In this paragraph, notice how the writer has made the order of events clear without using key words.

> Gracie's week in Italy was not what she hoped it would be. For the first three days, it rained. When the rain finally stopped, Gracie went for a walk and twisted her ankle. On her last night, she went out for a lovely dinner. But when she came back to the hotel, she found a mouse in her bed. Then on the flight home her luggage was lost.

In this paragraph, the writer describes steps without relying on key words.

> It's important to plan for a camping trip carefully. About a month before you go, look at maps. Get to know the trail you will be taking. About a week before the trip, begin packing the things you'll need. The day before your trip date, check on the weather. You may need a raincoat.

Read the paragraph. Then choose the correct answer to each question.

> Nita Taylor, ten years old, was walking her dog Rollo last week. Rollo saw a groundhog and chased it down a rocky slope. Nita started after the dog, but she slipped. She tumbled down the slope and got her foot caught in an old fence. When Rollo saw that she couldn't get up, he ran up the hill, barking. He barked at the door of their house. Nita's father came out. Rollo led Mr. Taylor down the slope to rescue Nita.

1. What happened just after Nita slipped?

   A Her dog Rollo saw a groundhog.

   B She started down the slope after her dog.

   C She tumbled down the slope and got her foot caught in an old fence.

2. What happened right before Nita's father came out of the house?

   F Rollo led Mr. Taylor down the slope to rescue Nita.

   G Rollo saw a groundhog and chased it down a rocky slope.

   H Rollo barked at the door of the house.

Each paragraph below tells a story or describes a process. Each paragraph is missing one sentence. Read each paragraph. Then choose its missing event or step from among the four lettered sentences. Write the letter of that sentence on the line.

A He went to the kitchen and started the coffeemaker.

B She unscrewed the lug nuts and removed the tire.

C Now he's training for the Thanksgiving Day Marathon.

D Then she took the bus to work.

1. Emily couldn't find her wallet, so she retraced her steps of the day. In the morning, she bought coffee at the corner store. _____. She didn't use her wallet at lunchtime, because she had brought a sandwich. Her friend Henry gave her a ride home, and they stopped at a tollbooth. Emily paid the toll. She must have left her wallet in Henry's car.

2. As she was driving home, Boki's tire went flat. She pulled off the road and inspected the tire. It had been punctured by a nail. She got the jack out of her trunk and set it up. _____. Then she put the spare tire on and replaced the lug nuts. She tossed the punctured tire into the trunk to be patched later. She still made it home in time for dinner.

3. Hugh got up at 6:00 A.M. on his mother's birthday. _____. When the coffee was almost done, he heated up a frying pan and cooked scrambled eggs. At 6:20 he put two slices of bread into the toaster. By the time his mother's alarm went off, Hugh was standing by her bed with a full breakfast on a tray.

4. On the first of January, Nikos decided to get fit. He jogged halfway around the pond but got tired. He walked the rest of the way around. By the end of January, he could jog all the way around the pond. By early April, he was running twice around the pond every morning. It was too hot to run outdoors when summer came, so Nikos used the treadmill at the gym. _____.

C ▶ Apply

Read each topic sentence. Then read the four supporting sentences below it. Number these sentences from 1 to 4 in time order.

1. Roasting marshmallows can be the best part of camping.

    _____ When it is brown and crisp, pull it off and eat it!

    _____ Roast the marshmallow just above the flames of the fire.

    _____ Find a long, thin stick.

    _____ Put a fresh marshmallow on the end of the stick.

2. Kittens need to be properly weaned before you give them away.

    _____ When it's three or four weeks old, the kitten can start eating solid, wet food.

    _____ When a kitten is newborn, it should only drink its mother's milk.

    _____ After two weeks, you can dip your finger in milk and let the kitten lick it off. Then you can give it a saucer of milk.

    _____ After seven or eight weeks, it will be ready to go to its new home.

3. The clothing of women in Europe has changed over the years.

    _____ In the 16th century, women's vests were made stiff with whalebone.

    _____ Today, European women wear dresses, slacks, jeans, or sweatpants: whatever suits them!

    _____ Women wore tight corsets until the late 1800s.

    _____ In the 1920s, they started wearing short skirts instead of long ones.

4. The artist in the park can do your portrait in 15 minutes or it's free.

    _____ When he has gotten your features right, he puts in highlights and shadows so that you don't look flat.

    _____ He spends the last few minutes drawing your hair. Voilà!

    _____ He spends about five minutes total on your eyes, nose, and mouth.

    _____ He begins by sketching the general shape of your head.

◆D Check Up

The details in the following paragraphs are presented in time order. In each paragraph, one sentence is missing. Read each paragraph. Then choose the sentence that belongs on the line.

1. Claude and Tabitha spent a day climbing Bald Mountain. They began their climb at sunrise. They hiked all morning, stopping only for bathroom breaks. At noon they stopped for a half-hour lunch. They were tired by late afternoon, so they sang songs to keep their spirits up. _____.

    A They packed plenty of water for their hike.

    B Their sandwiches were soggy, but they tasted good.

    C They mapped out their trail the night before the climb.

    D As the sun was going down, they reached the peak and happily set up camp.

2. The pirate Jack Bones raided the ship *Queen Anne* off the coast of Spain. He took $50,000 worth of gold. With his stolen treasure, he sailed down to North Africa. He buried the gold on a beach in Morocco. _____. Six months later, another pirate set fire to Jack's ship. Jack died, and the map was destroyed. No one has ever found the gold.

    F Jack tried to escape the burning ship but had no lifeboat.

    G He drew a map of the treasure site.

    H He got his name from an older pirate.

    J The captain of the *Queen Anne* fought bravely.

3. Sam goes to acting class every Wednesday. Each class begins with all the students yelling as loud as they can for five minutes. The teacher says that good yelling loosens you up for good acting. _____. When they are done, they sit in a circle and talk about how the scenes could be better.

    A Once they're loosened up, the students act out scenes.

    B On Tuesdays, Sam studies Russian.

    C They have to take off their shoes before they enter the room.

    D Next term, Sam will try to write a play.

Identifying the Unrelated Sentence

All the sentences in a paragraph should relate to its main idea. The main idea may be stated in a topic sentence. The supporting sentences give details about that idea. If a sentence does not relate directly to the main idea, it should be removed.

Notice how all the sentences in the following paragraph work together. The first sentence is the topic sentence. It tells readers that the Internet helps travelers. Sentences 2, 3, and 4 give details about ways the Internet helps.

> The Internet can be a great help in travel planning. Within minutes you can buy discount airline tickets. You can reserve a room at a hotel. Some sites even offer dollars-off coupons for attractions you might enjoy.

In the next paragraph, the main idea is not directly stated. However, all the sentences except one tell about Travis's bad experience this morning. The underlined sentence does not develop that main idea. It should be removed.

> Travis remembered why he hated city driving. First, he got stuck in a traffic jam on the freeway. Travis drives a compact car. Getting off at the wrong exit, he became lost on one-way streets. When he got to his building, there was no place to park. Next time, he will take the bus.

Read the paragraph. Then choose the correct answer to each question.

> She's a little old for toys, but Ali collects dolls anyway. These are not just any dolls, though. They are characters from popular movies. As a child, Ali really enjoyed *Cinderella*. The dolls must be in their unopened boxes. Ali hopes that someday doll collectors will make her rich.

1. What is the main idea of the paragraph?

   A Ali enjoyed *Cinderella*.

   B Ali collects dolls.

   C Collectors may pay top dollar for popular dolls.

2. Which sentence does not tell more about the main idea?

   F These are not just any dolls, though.

   G Ali hopes that someday doll collectors will make her rich.

   H As a child, Ali really enjoyed *Cinderella*.

◆B Practice

One sentence in each paragraph below does not belong. Cross out that sentence. On the line, explain why that sentence should be deleted.

1. Why was Jimmy Stewart such a popular movie star? He seemed just like us, only better. Stewart was born in 1908. He usually played ordinary men who tried hard to do the right thing. His characters faced trouble. But they came through with honesty, grace, and humor.

    The crossed-out sentence doesn't belong because

    _____

2. To Lynn, summertime meant one thing: the pool. Every morning, she went to the pool early. She gave swimming lessons. In the afternoon, she worked as a lifeguard. Lifeguards must pass difficult tests. Before going home, she always swam a few laps just for fun.

    The crossed-out sentence doesn't belong because

    _____

3. Joe is looking for a new job. His brother has a job at the garage. Joe checks the want ads every day. He sends applications to local businesses. He has updated his resume. If Joe keeps up the effort, he is sure to land a job soon.

    The crossed-out sentence doesn't belong because

    _____

4. The garden was lovely all year. During winter, the fir trees stood out against the white snow. With spring came tulips and flowering trees. Summer brought roses and day lilies. Fall was time for the wild colors of dahlias. Flowers need plenty of water and sunlight.

    The crossed-out sentence doesn't belong because

    _____

Read each of the following paragraphs. If all the sentences are related to the main idea, write *Correct* on the line. If one sentence is unrelated, cross it out.

1. Deep-piled rugs lay on gleaming hardwood floors. I am glad that I don't have to clean those floors. Dark velvet curtains covered the windows. At one side of the room was an old piano. The flowers in vases around the room sent a sweet smell into the air. Light twinkled from a crystal chandelier. The whole room sent a message of calm and luxury.

    _____

2. People often do strange things. Think about those who bought pet rocks during the 1970s. They spent good money on rocks! Soil is made up of tiny bits of rock. They gave their rocks names. They carried their "pets" around in boxes with breathing holes. This fad lasted only a short time. But it proved that people will do almost anything to fit in with the crowd.

    _____

3. Will is a model railroad lover. Go down into his basement and you enter a special world. Basements can be damp and chilly. There he has laid a network of tracks around a tiny city. He'll be glad to get the train going for you. It will go past the courthouse, over the bridge, and through the park. Will thinks his creation is worth every minute he has put into it.

    _____

4. Each lighthouse looks unique. One lighthouse might be white with red stripes. The next one down the coast might be all white. They are different for a good reason. By being different, they helped sailors know where they were. Sailors would see a lighthouse. Then they would check a list. The list would tell them the location of the lighthouse that matched that description.

    _____

5. Each family member is proud of a special skill. George knows all the words to songs by the Beatles. Blake can make pizza. Robin can wiggle her ears. Alice enjoys swing dancing. Swing was popular in the 1940s. What a strange family!

    _____

D ▶ Check Up

Read each paragraph. Then circle the letter of the sentence that does not belong.

1.   **1.** If you want to save dollars, watch your pennies. **2.** Pennies are made of zinc that is coated with copper. **3.** Pack your lunch instead of eating out. **4.** Resolve to buy clothes on sale and never at full price.

   A Sentence 1

   B Sentence 2

   C Sentence 3

   D Sentence 4

2.   **1.** The boa constrictor's favorite food is bats. **2.** To catch a bat, the boa hangs from vines. **3.** When a bat flies at night, it may bump into a waiting boa. **4.** The boa wraps itself around the bat and squeezes it to death. **5.** Many people think bats are creepy.

   F Sentence 1

   G Sentence 3

   H Sentence 4

   J Sentence 5

3.   **1.** When you need to stay awake, have a cup of coffee. **2.** The caffeine in the coffee revs up the nervous system. **3.** Today, most grocery stores sell decaf coffee. **4.** Caffeine makes the brain work faster and keeps you alert.

   A Sentence 1

   B Sentence 2

   C Sentence 3

   D Sentence 4

4.   **1.** Most Americans love the Statue of Liberty. **2.** She raises her lamp in New York Harbor. **3.** New York City has many interesting sites. **4.** The huge statue stands for freedom for all.

   F Sentence 1

   G Sentence 2

   H Sentence 3

   J Sentence 4

Main Idea and Topic Sentence

A **paragraph** is a group of sentences. The sentences work together to tell about a single idea. The most important idea in a paragraph is called the **main idea.** In many paragraphs, the main idea is stated in a single sentence. This sentence is called the **topic sentence.**

The topic sentence can appear anywhere in a paragraph. As the first sentence, it leads readers into the paragraph. Toward the middle or end, it can restate what has come before.

Supporting Sentences

The topic sentence states the main idea. Other sentences in the paragraph tell more about the main idea. They are called **supporting sentences.**

Supporting sentences can develop a paragraph in many ways. In descriptive paragraphs, supporting sentences may give **sensory details.** In other types of paragraphs, the supporting sentences may give **examples, facts and figures,** or **reasons.**

Sequence

Many paragraphs present details in **time order.** Sometimes, but not always, writers use key words to show the order of events. Some of those key words are *first, second, next, then, last,* and *finally.*

Unrelated Sentences

All the sentences in a paragraph should relate to the main idea. If the main idea is stated in a topic sentence, the other sentences should develop that idea. When there is no topic sentence, all the sentences should develop a single main idea. When you write paragraphs, edit carefully. Remove any sentence that does not tell about the main idea.

Read each paragraph below. Circle the letter of the sentence that best fills in the blank in the paragraph.

1. _____. First, she fastens her seat belt. She locks the doors. Then she checks the rearview mirror. Finally, she turns the key and starts the engine. She feels ready to drive.

   A Drivers must follow the rules of the road.

   B Mariah drives to work every day.

   C Mariah goes through a regular routine before she drives.

   D A good driver is a careful driver.

2. _____. A good laugh can improve your mental outlook. Laughing releases good chemicals into the body. It can even lower your blood pressure.

   F Laughter is good for us in many ways.

   G Some people rarely laugh.

   H Why do jokes make people laugh?

   J Children laugh more often than adults.

3. Henry wheeled his mower off the truck. _____. Then he threw the cut grass into a big pile. Before driving away, he left his bill with the homeowner.

   A He rolled his mower back onto the truck.

   B First, he mowed the lawn.

   C He drove to his next job.

   D First, he stopped for lunch.

4. Georgia O'Keeffe was born in 1887. _____. Later, she went to art college. In college she won prizes for her fine work.

   F Critics noticed how creative her work was.

   G Her college teachers showed her new ways to paint.

   H After college, she became famous for her flower paintings.

   J As a young girl, she took painting lessons.

Read each topic sentence. Then choose the answer that best develops the topic sentence.

5. Experts say that it is not likely that aliens are visiting Earth.

    F A UFO is an Unidentified Flying Object. Reports say that UFOs are shaped like saucers.

    G There have been reports that UFOs have been seen on Earth. Some people say that small creatures fly the UFOs.

    H They say that no alien even knows we are here. Also, they can't see any reason why aliens would want to come to Earth.

    J There are about 400 billion stars in Earth's home galaxy. There may be 400 billion other galaxies.

6. It is fast and easy to buy things from a catalog.

    A Those who lived in rural areas used to buy items from catalogs. They had problems getting to good stores.

    B You can call an 800 number to place your order. You know right away if it is in stock. Then you wait for the item to come to you.

    C The price you pay may be good. But remember that most states charge a sales tax.

    D Today some companies have switched to online catalogs. To see them, you need a computer.

7. The German shepherd makes a good police dog.

    F Dachshunds are not big enough to do the job. They also cannot be counted on to follow directions.

    G Some police dogs help police do their jobs at airports. They can sniff out drugs in baggage.

    H Trainers start working with dogs early. They begin when the dogs are still puppies.

    J German shepherds are big and strong. Because they are smart, they can be trained easily. Also, they are loyal and gentle.

Read each paragraph. Then choose the sentence that does not belong in the paragraph.

8.　　**1.** Diamonds are judged by how clear and big they are. **2.** A perfectly clear diamond is rare and expensive. **3.** Big diamonds are worth more than little ones. **4.** Some say the Hope diamond is cursed.

　　A Sentence 1

　　B Sentence 2

　　C Sentence 3

　　D Sentence 4

9.　　**1.** An angry dog can be a real danger. **2.** If you come face to face with an angry dog, stand still. **3.** Dogs wag their tails when they are happy. **4.** Speak to the dog calmly and in a quiet voice.

　　F Sentence 1

　　G Sentence 2

　　H Sentence 3

　　J Sentence 4

10.　　**1.** Terry uses her creativity at the day care center. **2.** She writes her own songs every day. **3.** She makes up games for the children to play. **4.** The children at the center are three to five years old.

　　A Sentence 1

　　B Sentence 2

　　C Sentence 3

　　D Sentence 4

11.　　**1.** The café was really crowded. **2.** All the booths and the tables were taken. **3.** Downtown is famous for having plenty of good restaurants. **4.** The counter was full. **5.** There was even a line of people waiting for places to sit.

　　F Sentence 2

　　G Sentence 3

　　H Sentence 4

　　J Sentence 5

Capitalizing Proper Nouns

Capital letters call attention to certain special words. There are a number of rules for capitalizing words.

Capitalize the names of people. Begin every word and initial in a person's name with a capital letter. Put a period after every initial.

Martin Luther King   Susan B. Anthony

Many people have titles before their names. There are short forms, or abbreviations, for many titles. **Capitalize titles and their abbreviations when you use them with names.**

General Scott   President Adams

Dr. Otis   Mrs. Lopez

Capitalize words for family relations when they are used with or in place of the names of specific people. (Do not capitalize words for family relations when they follow possessive pronouns such as *my*, *our*, or *your*.)

Mom will come with us.   My mom will come with us.

Grandpa Joe built houses.   Our grandpa built houses.

Uncle Frank phoned.   Your uncle phoned.

Underline the words in each sentence that should be capitalized.

1. Have you met mrs. helen jacobs?

2. The package is being sent to e. h. yates.

3. I remember uncle milton always told the best jokes.

4. Both mr. and mrs. fulton work at the restaurant.

5. Tell aunt sonya to call dr. harris in the morning.

6. I spoke to mayor henson at the meeting.

7. The band played marches by john philip sousa.

8. Ask ms. moore all your questions about the new computer.

9. I see joyce, leann, and stacy every day on the bus.

10. The award was given to coach rodriguez.

B ▸ Practice

Read each of the following items. Capitalize words wherever necessary. Write *Correct* if the item is written properly.

1. mrs. karen robinson   _____

2. my cousin   _____

3. senator barbara glenn   _____

4. Jackson a. Perkins   _____

5. aunt Diana   _____

6. queen Elizabeth   _____

7. captain paul d. daniels   _____

8. one mayor   _____

9. dr. carl williams   _____

10. carla m. ramirez   _____

Read each of the following pairs of sentences. Circle the letter of the sentence in each pair that is capitalized correctly.

11. **A** This quilt was sewn by grandma ruth.

    B This quilt was sewn by Grandma Ruth.

12. **A** Only one Man, franklin d. roosevelt, was elected President four times.

    B Only one man, Franklin D. Roosevelt, was elected president four times.

13. **A** The name of my new doctor is Dr. Timothy Newell.

    B The name of my new Doctor is dr. Timothy Newell.

14. **A** The telephone call is from ms. Jessica Carlson.

    B The telephone call is from Ms. Jessica Carlson.

C Apply

Rewrite each of the following sentences with correct capitalization.

1. Are you here to see mr. l. b. taylor or mr. j. f. taylor?

   _____

2. This story was written by a. a. milne.

   _____

3. Last week I had dinner with aunt josie and uncle george.

   _____

4. Will dr. lee please come to the front desk?

   _____

5. Give the letter to ms. sara brenner.

   _____

6. There is a picture of governor keller in the newspaper.

   _____

7. Did aunt doris get the tools that belonged to our grandfather?

   _____

8. This is the office of judge kathleen marshall.

   _____

9. I enjoyed the book by robert l. stevenson.

   _____

10. She, marcella, and kim share an office.

    _____

D Check Up

For each item, choose the sentence that is capitalized correctly.

1. **A** Please return these forms to mrs. Croce.

   B May I speak to Dr. Schultz?

   C I bought my new car from Mr. hayes.

   D Is ms. wyman your Neighbor?

2. **F** You have a meeting with James t. Costa tomorrow.

   G The best bakery in town is owned by e. f. Cummings.

   H A vote for R. D. Michaels is a vote for progress!

   J The Principal at my son's school is Jana s. Carter.

3. **A** Are these the roses that Cousin David grew?

   B I hear that my Uncle has a new job.

   C The museum has a painting by grandma moses.

   D My Aunt loves folk dancing.

4. **F** The meeting notes were taken by secretary allen.

   G Stand when the Judge enters the courtroom.

   H Listen to the tips from Coach Sweeney.

   J I wrote a letter to governor Boyle.

Read each sentence and look at the underlined words. Choose the answer that is written correctly for the underlined words.

5. I think <u>grandpa flanders</u> is watching the game.

   A grandpa Flanders

   B Grandpa Flanders

   C Grandpa flanders

   D Correct as it is

6. A reporter talked to <u>Senator Jennings</u>.

   F senator Jennings

   G Senator jennings

   H senator jennings

   J Correct as it is

7. Always take your car to <u>a. j. Gordon</u> for repairs!

   A A. J. gordon

   B a. j. gordon

   C A. J. Gordon

   D Correct as it is

8. Will <u>mrs. barton</u> report to the office?

   F Mrs. barton

   G Mrs. Barton

   H mrs. Barton

   J Correct as it is

Capitalizing Proper Nouns and Proper Adjectives

Capitalize names of days, holidays, and months.

Sunday   Memorial Day   May

Capitalize the names of cities, states, and countries.

Miami   New York   Ireland

Capitalize the names of streets, buildings, and bridges.

High Street   Lincoln Memorial   Brooklyn Bridge

Capitalize geographical names.

Rocky Mountains   Grand Canyon   Snake River

The names of particular places and things may have more than one word. Capitalize all important words. Do not capitalize *the*, *of*, or *in*.

Capitalize proper adjectives. A proper adjective is an adjective formed from a proper noun.

Swedish meatballs   Olympic trials

Underline the words in each sentence that should be capitalized.

1. The halloween party will be on friday, october 31.

2. The meet will be held at granada high school on wall street.

3. Someday I want to climb the eiffel tower in paris, france.

4. We took a houseboat down the ohio river.

5. Marie took a class in french cooking.

6. The colors of the painted desert in arizona are surprising.

7. My office building is on huron avenue.

8. I bought this russian doll at a department store in new york.

9. On labor day in september, the american people honor all workers.

10. At niagara falls, the niagara river drops almost 200 feet.

B Practice

Rewrite each term that is not written correctly. Capitalize words wherever necessary. Write *Correct* if the item is written properly.

1. monday   _____

2. city   _____

3. canada   _____

4. rodeo drive   _____

5. atlantic ocean _____

6. swiss   _____

7. nebraska   _____

8. months   _____

Read each of the following pairs of sentences. Circle the letter of the sentence in each pair that is capitalized correctly.

9. **A** We took a vacation to yellowstone national park in August.

   B We took a vacation to Yellowstone National Park in August.

10. **A** Is the clearview Library on Oak street?

    B Is the Clearview Library on Oak Street?

11. **A** We are going to a picnic on the Fourth Of July.

    B We are going to a picnic on the Fourth of July.

12. **A** We ate at an Italian restaurant last night.

    B We ate at an italian restaurant last Night.

13. **A** Many people try to climb Mount Everest in the country of Nepal.

    B Many people try to climb Mount everest in the Country of nepal.

14. **A** My brother lives in anchorage, alaska.

    B My brother lives in Anchorage, Alaska.

C Apply

Rewrite each of the following sentences with correct capitalization.

1. I start my new job on tuesday, june 4.

2. We can meet at the corner of collins drive and concord road.

3. Were the chinese people the first to make paper?

4. The sport of surfing began in hawaii.

5. Be sure to visit the statue of liberty when you are in new york city.

6. The city of chicago, illinois, is next to lake michigan.

7. We celebrate thanksgiving in november.

8. The thames river flows through london, england.

9. I have to work one saturday every month.

10. Many people in mexico speak both the spanish and the english language.

For each item, choose the sentence that is capitalized correctly.

1. **A** A famous battle took place in gettysburg, Pennsylvania.

   B We camped at Yosemite National Park.

   C My neighbor moved to St. Louis, missouri.

   D Last Summer we visited crater lake.

2. **F** Did you know that Rhode island is the smallest State in the United states?

   G The first Monday in September is labor day.

   H We ate with chopsticks at the Vietnamese restaurant.

   J The Store is on Euclid Avenue.

3. **A** My parents came from Lagos, Nigeria.

   B I visited the zoo in San diego, California.

   C Your appointment is on thursday, may 2.

   D The Nile River is the longest River in the World.

4. **F** Come to our Party for the Chinese new year!

   G The Great Salt Lake is saltier than the Oceans.

   H There was an accident on my Street.

   J My insurance bill is due on Friday, October 14.

Read each sentence and look at the underlined words. Choose the answer that is written correctly for the underlined words.

5. Our plane landed in <u>atlanta, Georgia</u>.

   A Atlanta, georgia

   B atlanta, georgia

   C Atlanta, Georgia

   D Correct as it is

6. The sale starts on <u>wednesday, march 20</u>.

   F Wednesday, march 20

   G Wednesday, March 20

   H wednesday, March 20

   J Correct as it is

Capitalizing First Words and Titles

Begin every sentence with a capital letter.

>   The letter is on the desk. Who sent the letter?

Capitalize the first word of every direct quotation.

>   "What time is it?" asked Ray.
>   Ken said, "It's noon."

Capitalize the first word, the last word, and any other important words in a title. Do not capitalize *a, an, by, for, from, in,* or *the* unless it comes first or last.

When the titles of long works such as books, movies, plays, and magazines are printed in books, they appear in italics. When the titles of short works such as stories, poems, or television programs are printed in books, they are put into quotation marks.

>   *The Eye of the World* (book)
>   *The Silence of the Lambs* (movie)
>   "The Gift of the Magi" (short story)

Underline the words in each sentence that should be capitalized.

1. "remember to bring your jacket," said the coach.

2. the waiter asked, "what would you like to drink?"

3. my friend said that *howl's moving castle* is a funny book.

4. where is the cafeteria?

5. most children love the story "the three billy goats gruff."

6. the driver ordered, "move to the back of the bus!"

7. "the singers in *the phantom of the opera* are great," wrote the reviewer.

8. "how long have you worked here?" asked the new boss.

9. Kit said, "one of my favorite movies is *beauty and the beast.*"

10. Ben cut out an article called "building a deck" from *your garden and home.*

B Practice

Rewrite each title that is not written correctly. Capitalize words as needed. Write *Correct* if the item is written properly.

1. *the last of the mohicans* (movie) _____

2. "by the waters of Babylon" (short story) _____

3. "the raven" (poem) _____

4. *The Return of the King* (book) _____

5. "all in the family" (TV program) _____

6. *house and garden* (magazine) _____

7. *The Miracle Worker* (play) _____

8. *The catcher in the Rye* (book) _____

Read each of the following pairs of sentences. Circle the letter of the sentence in each pair that is capitalized correctly.

9. **A** "this radio does not work," said Blake.

   B "This radio does not work," said Blake.

10. **A** The clerk said, "please sign your name."

    B The clerk said, "Please sign your name."

11. **A** the flowers in this garden are lovely.

    B The flowers in this garden are lovely.

12. **A** "The weather will be cloudy," said the newscaster.

    B "the weather will be cloudy," said the newscaster.

13. **A** Apple pie is a popular dessert.

    B apple pie is a popular dessert.

14. **A** The reporter asked, "How did the fire begin?"

    B The reporter asked, "how did the fire begin?"

Rewrite each of the following sentences with correct capitalization.

1. did you watch "law and order" last night?

   _____

2. we enjoy the stories in *reader's digest*.

   _____

3. the umpire yelled, "strike three!"

   _____

4. many people think *citizen kane* is a great movie.

   _____

5. the zoo keeper told us, "the lion cub is only one month old."

   _____

6. "brush your teeth twice a day," said the dentist.

   _____

7. we read the poem "stopping by woods on a snowy evening."

   _____

8. "how much does this shirt cost?" asked the customer.

   _____

9. my boss said, "mail these letters."

   _____

10. "this bus is always late," complained the passengers.

   _____

D Check Up

Read the sentences below. For each item, choose the sentence that is capitalized correctly.

1. **A** "my car has a flat tire," said my neighbor.

   B "My trip begins tomorrow,"my sister said.

   C the tourist asked, "will you take me to the hotel?"

   D The teacher said, "memorize the poem."

2. **F** "take the medicine twice a day," said the doctor.

   G everyone remarked, "How hot it is today!"

   H "Be careful," the police officer reminded us.

   J The cab driver asked, "where do you want to go?"

3. **A** My brother has seen *Star Wars* about twenty times.

   B Have you ever read *Call Of The Wild*?

   C the story "Beware Of The Dog" has a surprise ending.

   D We watch "the Simpsons" every week.

4. **F** "this chair is too hard," complained the little girl.

   G The cook said, "the soup needs more salt."

   H the salesclerk told me, "You look great in this dress!"

   J "Always do your best," the coach told her team.

Read each sentence and look at the underlined words. Choose the answer that is written correctly for the underlined words.

5. <u>*War and Peace*</u> is very long.

   A *war and peace*

   B *War And Peace*

   C *War and peace*

   D Correct as it is

6. <u>my neighbor said, "your</u> dog barks too much."

   F My neighbor said, "Your

   G my neighbor said, "Your

   H My neighbor said, "your

   J Correct as it is

7. <u>My son asked, "can</u> you drive me to the store?"

   A my son asked, "can

   B my son asked, "Can

   C My son asked, "Can

   D Correct as it is

8. I love <u>*singin' in the rain*</u>.

   F *Singin' In The Rain*

   G *Singin' in the Rain*

   H *Singin' in the rain*

   J Correct as it is

Review

Proper Nouns and Proper Adjectives

Capitalize the names of people. Capitalize titles and their abbreviations.

    Mary Lou Retton   Captain Prescott   Dr. Santos

Capitalize words for family relations when they are used with or in place of the names of specific people.

    Grandpa George   Aunt Sally   my dad

Capitalize the names of days, holidays, and months.

    Thursday   Thanksgiving   November

Capitalize the names of cities, states, and countries.

    Portland   Kansas   Brazil

Capitalize the names of streets, buildings, and bridges.

    Grant Avenue   Carnegie Library   Key Bridge

Capitalize geographical names.

    Crater Lake   Mount Rainier   Atlantic Ocean

Capitalize proper adjectives.

    African mask   Oriental rug   Martian canal

First Words

Begin every sentence with a capital letter.

    Are you hungry? My sister baked some cookies.

Capitalize the first word of every direct quotation.

    "Where is my book?" asked Dave.

    Sherri answered, "Your book is on the shelf."

Titles

Capitalize the first, last, and any other important words in a title.

    All Quiet on the Western Front (book and movie)

    "The Lady or the Tiger" (short story)

    "Hail to the Chief" (song)

Read the paragraphs and look at the numbered, underlined parts. Choose the answer that is written correctly for each underlined part.

(1)   The <u>state of washington</u> was named in honor of
(2) <u>george washington</u>. It is famous for its beautiful scenery. It has high
(3) mountains and huge forests. The state lies on the <u>pacific ocean</u>.

1. **A** State of Washington
   B state of Washington
   C State of washington
   D Correct as it is

3. **A** Pacific Ocean
   B Pacific ocean
   C pacific Ocean
   D Correct as it is

2. **F** George washington
   G george Washington
   H George Washington
   J Correct as it is

(4)   <u>Robert louis stevenson</u> was a well-known 19th century
(5) novelist. This <u>scottish writer</u> loved the sea. Though he was
       trained as a lawyer, he preferred writing. School children all
(6) over the world read his book <u>*Treasure Island*</u> about adventure
       on the high seas.

4. **F** Robert louis Stevenson
   G Robert Louis Stevenson
   H robert louis Stevenson
   J Correct as it is

6. **F** *Treasure island*
   G *treasure Island*
   H *treasure island*
   J Correct as it is

5. **A** Scottish Writer
   B Scottish writer
   C scottish Writer
   D Correct as it is

(7)   <u>my Family</u> loves to celebrate unusual holidays. Our favorite is

(8) <u>April Fools' Day</u>. On that day, you had better stay away from
Uncle Alex. He loves to play tricks!

7.
- A My Family
- B My family
- C my family
- D Correct as it is

8.
- F april fools' day
- G April Fools' day
- H April fools' Day
- J Correct as it is

(9)   I had just moved to <u>san jose, California</u>. I was looking for

(10) <u>Sonoma street</u>, but I was lost. Imagine how relieved I was

(11) when a woman stopped and asked <u>me, "can</u> I help you?" She gave
me the directions I needed.

9.
- F San Jose, california
- G San Jose, California
- H San jose, California
- J Correct as it is

11.
- F me, "Can
- G Me, "can
- H Me, "Can
- J Correct as it is

10.
- A sonoma street
- B sonoma Street
- C Sonoma Street
- D Correct as it is

(12)   <u>Last monday</u> I was shopping at the mall. As I passed a pet shop,

(13) I saw a lovely <u>persian cat</u> in the window. I just had to buy her.
Even my vet, Dr. Joslin, says she is one of the most beautiful cats
she has ever seen. I am very lucky!

12.
- A Last Monday
- B last monday
- C last Monday
- D Correct as it is

13.
- F Persian cat
- G Persian Cat
- H persian Cat
- J Correct as it is

For each item, choose the sentence with correct capitalization.

14. F Have you ever seen the movie *Lawrence Of Arabia?*

    G We planted trees on Arbor day.

    H Send the package to 489 East Avenue.

    J You can see dr. Connors now.

15. A We are going to Grandma Anna's house for dinner.

    B Turn left on the next Street.

    C Your books are due on thursday.

    D My company has a picnic every Summer.

16. F You can rent canoes at lake Williams.

    G Do you like italian food?

    H The teacher said, "open your books."

    J The train makes a stop in Topeka, Kansas.

17. A The museum will be closed all Month.

    B can you drive me to the Store?

    C She and aunt Connie work together.

    D My neighbor moved to Texas.

18. F You can pick up your photos on Friday.

    G The River floods almost every Spring.

    H We are taking a vacation in july.

    J My father and mr. Harris are old friends.

19. A The wall is decorated with spanish tiles.

    B We took some great pictures in Monument Valley.

    C I had the flu last february.

    D There are free concerts every tuesday.

20. F The clerk asked, "What is your address?"

    G Joe works at uncle Tony's store.

    H The story took place in a little german town.

    J My children enjoy books written by e.b. White.

21. A Many people buy cards on Valentine's day.

    B We hiked in bryce national Park.

    C She works for Mayor Hopkins.

    D You cannot park your car on this Street.

End Marks

Period

Use a period at the end of a statement.

> There are 366 days in a leap year.

Use a period at the end of most commands.

> Call me tomorrow.

Question Mark

Use a question mark at the end of a question.

> What is your name?

Exclamation Point

Use an exclamation point at the end of exclamatory sentences.

> We won the game!

Use an exclamation point at the end of a command that shows strong feeling.

> Watch out!

Write a period, a question mark, or an exclamation point at the end of each sentence.

1. What time is your appointment

2. Sign your name on the dotted line

3. How hungry I am

4. Call the police

5. I usually ride my bike to work

6. Close the door quietly on your way out

7. What time does the movie begin

8. Get out of the way

9. Mr. Harris opened an account at the bank

10. What an exciting game that was

B Practice

For each sentence, decide which end mark is needed.

1. We planted tomatoes in our garden

   A .   **B** ?   **C** !

2. Would you like a sample of our new ice cream

   F .   **G** ?   **H** !

3. Run for cover

   A .   **B** ?   **C** !

4. Nathan shouted, "Hurry up"

   F .   **G** ?   **H** !

5. When will you finish this job

   A .   **B** ?   **C** !

6. Put the papers on the desk

   F .   **G** ?   **H** !

For each item, circle the letter of the sentence with the correct end mark.

7. **A** My grandfather made this cabinet many years ago.

   B My grandfather made this cabinet many years ago!

8. **A** Don't open that door!

   B Don't open that door?

9. **A** What a wonderful idea.

   B What a wonderful idea!

10. **A** Did I get any calls!

    B Did I get any calls?

11. **A** Be sure to dress warmly?

    B Be sure to dress warmly.

12. **A** Where can we buy a quick lunch!

    B Where can we buy a quick lunch?

C ▸ Apply

**Each of the following items describes a situation. For each situation, write
what you would say in one sentence. Use the correct end mark.**

1. You see a child about to touch a hot pot.

   _____

2. You see a news article you think your friend would like.

   _____

3. You are amazed at how strong the wind is.

   _____

4. You want to know which pizza toppings you should order.

   _____

5. You want someone to hand you a letter.

   _____

6. You see a house on fire.

   _____

7. A friend shows you his antique toy collection.

   _____

8. You want to know who is speaking at tonight's meeting.

   _____

9. You are describing the car of your dreams.

   _____

10. You see that a family member needs medical attention right now.

   _____

D Check Up

For each item, choose the sentence that has the correct end mark.

1. A How tired I feel?

   B May I speak to Mrs. Lee?

   C Probably the office you want is on your left!

   D Please follow me!

2. F What a great gift!

   G We are going to a concert?

   H Would you bake some cookies for our next bake sale.

   J How beautiful the scenery is?

3. A Who won the race.

   B How much experience do you have with computers!

   C We are moving to a new apartment?

   D My car has another flat tire!

4. F Ask the clerk for a copy of notes from the last meeting!

   G Please mail these letters!

   H The plane will land in ten minutes.

   J Where can I park my car.

5. A When does the store close.

   B How did the fire begin?

   C Please fasten your seat belts?

   D Run for cover.

6. F These are the most delicious cookies I have ever eaten?

   G What kind of dog do you own!

   H Football is a very popular sport?

   J Fill out these forms.

7. A Take a brownie for dessert!

   B Watch out for that falling ladder!

   C May I borrow your pen.

   D I can deliver your order tomorrow?

8. F Would you like to have dinner with me on Friday.

   G Stop making so much noise?

   H The daffodils in my garden are blooming.

   J What a scary movie that was?

For each sentence, decide which end mark is needed.

9. Would you like pancakes for breakfast

   A .   B ?   C !

10. The line begins by the cash register

    F .   G ?   H !

11. How great it was to see you last Sunday

    A .   B ?   C !

12. How much did the movie tickets cost

    F .   G ?   H !

Commas in Compound Sentences

Often two or more sentences that can stand alone are joined in one sentence. This type of sentence is called a **compound sentence.** Each part that can stand alone is an **independent clause.** Commas make compound sentences easier to understand.

> Monday was hot, and Tuesday was hotter. (two clauses)
>
> Monday was hot, Tuesday was hotter, but today is the
>
>   hottest day of all. (three clauses)

Use a comma between clauses connected by the words *and*, *or*, *nor*, *but*, or *for*. Place the comma after the first clause, before the connecting word.

> Sue enjoys hiking, but Ed likes swimming.

Do not overuse commas. For example, no comma is needed if *and*, *or*, *nor*, *but*, or *for* connects two subjects or two verbs.

> Ray and Lou are friends. (compound subject)
>
> They walked or ran the whole time. (compound verb)

For each item, circle the letter of the sentence that is punctuated correctly.

1. **A** Neither he, nor I wanted to clean the garage.

   B Neither he nor I wanted to clean the garage.

2. **A** Anne may paint the ceiling, or she will sand the woodwork.

   B Anne may paint the ceiling or, she will sand the woodwork.

3. **A** John wanted to leave yesterday, but he left today instead.

   B John wanted to leave yesterday but he left today instead.

4. **A** The rain ruined our day, for we had planned to go on a picnic.

   B The rain ruined our day for we had planned to go on a picnic.

5. **A** Some skilled workers upgrade, and sell old computers.

   B Some skilled workers upgrade and sell old computers.

6. **A** Memphis, and St. Louis are cities on the Mississippi River.

   B Memphis and St. Louis are cities on the Mississippi River.

B Practice

Read the paragraph below. Look at the parts that are numbered and underlined. Choose the answer that is written correctly for each underlined part.

(1)   Volunteering to assist others can be hard <u>work but</u> many men
(2) and women are willing to help. Some people read to <u>children, or</u> tutor
(3) them in math. <u>Adults, and</u> teens work as aides in hospitals. Others
(4) visit people in nursing <u>homes or</u> bring food to shut-ins. Helping
(5) hands always are needed. The pay may be <u>poor but</u> the rewards are great!

1. **A** work but,

   B work, but

   C Correct as it is

2. **F** children or

   G children or,

   H Correct as it is

3. **A** Adults and,

   B Adults and

   C Correct as it is

4. **F** homes, or

   G homes or,

   H Correct as it is

5. **A** poor, but

   B poor but,

   C Correct as it is

Read each sentence. Add a comma if it is needed, or write *Correct* if the sentence is punctuated properly.

6. Jill and Fern went to the mall. _____

7. The repair shop is closed but the gas pumps are open. _____

8. I will try to fix this myself or you may call a plumber. _____

9. My computer would not work and the phone did not stop ringing all day.

   _____

10. The squirrels ran up trees or scurried under bushes. _____

11. Nearly everyone ate pizza but a few guests chose tacos instead.

    _____

12. Ice covered the roads for a storm had passed through overnight.

    _____

C Apply

Read each sentence. Add a comma if it is needed. Place an *X* over any comma that is not needed. Write *Correct* if the sentence is punctuated properly.

1. Kevin rushed to the station, but the train had left. _____

2. Both Adams, and Jefferson served as U.S. presidents. _____

3. You may not leave work early nor may you take a longer lunch hour.

   _____

4. The street looked dark and gloomy but the park was filled with bright

   lights. _____

5. Does Oscar sing in the chorus, or play the piano? _____

6. No one went hungry that night for we had plenty of food for everyone.

   _____

7. The frightened dog turned, and quickly ran away. _____

8. Neither the storm nor the slippery roads kept us from leaving on time.

   _____

9. Gardening is very enjoyable, but reading is my favorite hobby.

   _____

10. Ranelle neither skis, nor skates. _____

11. Men, and women fainted in the extreme heat. _____

12. The house was completely empty and whatever we said echoed through the

    large rooms. _____

13. We sat on the hillside and watched the fireworks. _____

14. The tables were filled with ethnic foods and we sampled one of everything.

    _____

15. Maurice slept soundly all night for he had walked ten miles that day.

    _____

D ◆ Check Up

For each item, choose the sentence that is punctuated correctly.

1. **A** Nick, and Brian work with computers.

   B They write programs, or design web pages.

   C Their work keeps them busy, but they find time to relax.

   D They hunt, and fish in Canada.

2. **F** Orchids are beautiful flowers, but they are hard to grow.

   G My plants are not looking the best for the slugs have taken over the yard.

   H Manny waters, and weeds his garden daily.

   J Pansies, or petunias make a colorful border.

3. **A** Carpenter ants chewed through the wooden sill, and made nests there.

   B Neither soap, nor spray worked on the ants.

   C Both Ben, and I tried our best to remove the ants.

   D We called an expert, and she got rid of them.

4. **F** New York, and Maine are states on the east coast.

   G Tourists swim underwater, or sail near the shore.

   H Ohio and Michigan border the Great Lakes.

   J Texas is a large state but Alaska is larger.

Read each sentence and look at the underlined part. Choose the answer that is written correctly for the underlined part.

5. The coffee was <u>cold and</u> the doughnuts were stale.

   A cold, and

   B cold, and,

   C Correct as it is

6. Neither the <u>geese, nor</u> the ducks were scared of us.

   F geese nor,

   G geese nor

   H Correct as it is

7. Leave your muddy shoes outside the <u>door or</u> be prepared to mop!

   A door or,

   B door, or

   C Correct as it is

8. Kyle ran as fast as he <u>could, but</u> he didn't get there in time.

   F could but,

   G could, but,

   H Correct as it is

A Introduce

Commas in Series

Commas are used to separate words or short phrases that are written in a series of three or more. Place a comma after each item in the series except the last item.

> Peter, Alex, and Tito have formed a band.

> She bought a gallon of milk, a loaf of bread, and four apples at the store.

If all of the items in the series are joined by connecting words, do not use a comma.

> Should I plant lettuce or carrots or beans?

For each of the following items, add commas where they are needed. If a phrase is written correctly and does not need a comma, write *Correct* on the line.

1. dogs cats or birds _____

2. juicy plums ripe peaches and sweet cherries _____

3. exercised lifted weights and ran _____

4. cold and rainy and windy _____

5. Tim Tom Ray or Joe _____

6. tables or chairs or lamps _____

7. sodas milkshakes and malts _____

8. twirls jumps or spins _____

9. Mr. Tan Ms. Chung and Dr. Wang _____

10. lions tigers and leopards _____

B Practice

For each item, circle the letter of the sentence in which commas are used correctly.

1. **A** Emma grows corn, beans, and sugar beets on her farm.

   B Emma grows corn, beans and sugar beets, on her farm.

2. **A** We couldn't decide whether to drive bike, or walk around the island.

   B We couldn't decide whether to drive, bike, or walk around the island.

3. **A** Hill Smith, and Johnson are the lawyers in this office.

   B Hill, Smith, and Johnson are the lawyers in this office.

4. **A** Should we grill ribs, chicken, or hot dogs tonight?

   B Should we grill ribs, chicken, or hot dogs, tonight?

5. **A** The room had blue walls, a red ceiling, and yellow woodwork.

   B The room had blue walls, a red ceiling, and, yellow woodwork.

Read each sentence. Add commas wherever necessary. Write *Correct* if the sentence is correct as it is.

6. Have you filed the papers sorted the mail and typed the letters?

   _____

7. Neither Hank nor Bill nor Sam could find the wrench. _____

8. Huge piles of red yellow and orange leaves covered the ground.

   _____

9. Did they order roast beef fried chicken or baked ham? _____

10. Robins crows doves and blue jays fly in and out of my garden.

    _____

11. Bring a tent a sleeping bag and warm clothes for the camping trip.

    _____

C Apply

Read each of the following sentences. Place commas wherever they are needed.

1. Look for the dog in the shed under the porch or in the house.

2. Ali Ivan Chu and I are seeing a movie tonight.

3. Stand still look at the camera and smile!

4. Books papers and pencils covered the entire table.

5. The soil was a mixture of sand clay and loam.

6. There is a bank a pet shop and a video store at the mall.

7. My pockets are stuffed with gum candy and bus tokens.

8. I'm getting a scoop of chocolate vanilla or peach ice cream.

9. Get a dozen buns one loaf of bread or some bagels from the bakery.

10. The fans cheered waved and clapped when the team took the field.

11. Holly rented *The Wizard of Oz Mary Poppins* and *Willy Wonka and the Chocolate Factory*.

12. My dog is a terrier German shepherd and beagle mix.

13. Jack's mother father and brother are visiting him in Seattle.

Read each sentence. Add commas wherever necessary. Write *Correct* if the sentence is correct as it is.

14. Frank needs markers or gel pens or chalk to make the poster.

    _____

15. We hiked through the woods swam in the lake and cooked over the

    campfire. _____

16. Does the chair fit in the car the van or the truck? _____

D Check Up

For each item, choose the sentence in which commas are used correctly.

1. **A** Blue green and, peach are my favorite colors.

   B Our flag is red, white, and blue.

   C The chair had a beige, tan, and brown, pattern.

   D Yellow, purple and white, flowers lined the path.

2. **F** Send for the tool that slices dices, and minces anything.

   G Skaters were slipping, sliding, or falling, on the ice.

   H The old train whistled, tooted, and chugged along the track.

   J He paused, took a breath, and, then went on with his talk.

3. **A** Mary teaches fifth, sixth, and seventh grade math.

   B Three, four or five, extra people may be coming.

   C My son plays first second, or third base on the team.

   D Check for the mail at noon, one, and two, o'clock.

4. **F** Buy shrimp clams or crayfish at the dock.

   G Oranges, limes, and lemons grow in warm climates.

   H The farmer sold squash beets, and peppers at the market.

   J I like lettuce, carrots, and, bean sprouts, in my salad.

Read each sentence and look at the underlined part. Choose the answer that is written correctly for the underlined part.

5. We had <u>soup, salad, and dessert</u> with our meal.

   A soup salad, and dessert

   B soup, salad and dessert,

   C soup salad and dessert

   D Correct as it is

6. Did you visit <u>London, Paris and Rome</u> on your trip?

   F London, Paris, and Rome

   G London Paris, and Rome

   H London, Paris, and Rome,

   J Correct as it is

7. Please <u>plant water and feed</u> these seedlings.

   A plant, water, and feed,

   B plant, water and, feed

   C plant, water, and feed

   D Correct as it is

8. They sell <u>books, prints, and cards</u>.

   F books, prints and cards

   G books prints, and cards

   H books, prints, and, cards

   J Correct as it is

Other Uses of Commas

Some sentences start with a special word or phrase. Using a comma to set off this special word or phrase makes the sentence clearer.

Put a comma after *yes* or *no* if the word is used to answer a question or to comment on something.

> <u>No</u>, I won't be able to come.

Use a comma to separate a long phrase from the rest of the sentence.

> <u>To reach the mountain peak</u>, we climbed for three hours.

Short phrases of four words or less need a comma only if the sentence would be hard to understand without it.

> <u>For that matter</u>, what else could we have done?

> <u>After dinner</u> we watched a movie.

For each item, circle the letter of the sentence that is punctuated correctly.

1. **A** Yes that new song will be a hit.

   B Yes, that new song will be a hit.

2. **A** When lightning struck the power line, our lights dimmed.

   B When lightning struck the power line our lights dimmed.

3. **A** No, I have not seen the TV remote control.

   B No I have not seen the TV remote control.

4. **A** By nightfall we had set up camp.

   B By nightfall, we had set up camp.

5. **A** According to our records it's time to see the dentist.

   B According to our records, it's time to see the dentist.

6. **A** Leaning on her crutches for support, Sara climbed the stairs.

   B Leaning on her crutches for support Sara climbed the stairs.

7. **A** For one reason or another, we had forgotten the appointment.

   B For one reason or another we had forgotten the appointment.

B ► Practice

A sentence may directly address someone or something. That is, the sentence names the person or thing spoken to. The name of the person or thing being addressed must be set off with commas.

If the name begins the sentence, place a comma after it. If the name ends the sentence, put a comma before it. If the name is within the sentence, place commas both before and after it.

> Mr. Long, please step this way.
>
> Let's go for a walk, my friend.
>
> Did you notice, Julie, that you have a flat tire?

Circle the word or words of direct address in each sentence.

1. Dale, where are the keys to the car?

2. Have you decided, Paula, where you will go on vacation?

3. Ladies and gentlemen, please welcome our speaker.

4. These pictures of Mexico are great, Jen.

5. Brother, thanks for your help.

6. You silly dog, where did you bury my wallet?

Read each sentence. Add commas wherever they are needed.

7. Fetch the stick Spot.

8. After the long dry spell the rain was welcome.

9. In the bleacher seats fans baked in the sun.

10. Rachel is the coffee hot?

11. To see the country travel by bus or train.

12. Yes this is the office of Dr. Burns.

13. I'm afraid I can't come today Mrs. Rivers.

14. Due to the foggy weather the freeway is closed.

15. Your book sir is very well written.

C ▶ Apply

Rewrite each sentence. Add commas wherever they are needed.

1. Since the elevator was broken we had to use the stairs.

   _____

2. Yes the books came in the mail today Paul.

   _____

3. By the time we ate dinner it was too late to see the game.

   _____

4. Do you think Dan that the car can be fixed?

   _____

5. Would you like some lemonade Ms. Newman?

   _____

6. Carrying a heavy backpack the ranger trudged along the trail.

   _____

7. If it stops raining we can finish painting the porch Pete.

   _____

8. During breakfast the crew looked over the plans for the new kitchen.

   _____

9. Did you bring snacks Seth for today's morning break?

   _____

10. No my dear we can't buy everything we see.

    _____

D Check Up

For each item, choose the sentence in which commas are used correctly.

1. **A** Yes, I'll be happy to attend your party Jane.

   B Running to catch the bus, Carmen, almost lost her briefcase.

   C Hunter, did you see my glasses?

   D In the evening we, went dancing.

2. **F** No, Sonny finish one task before you start another.

   G By the way, did you remember to set the alarm?

   H Needing a break the staff went, to the coffee shop.

   J Tell me Laura, how does the novel end?

3. **A** Victor, and Rose Burke, please go to Gate 11.

   B Yes, I'm engaged to, Bob.

   C Laughing, and jumping the children raced along the beach.

   D Will you attend the sessions, Dr. Rogers, beginning after lunch?

4. **F** When the wasps flew at him, Alan quickly ran away.

   G During the baseball game, Joe, and Ed caught a foul ball.

   H No the train does not stop here anymore, ma'am.

   J Would you like to play cards, Granddad or read?

Read each sentence and look at the underlined part. Choose the answer that is written correctly for the underlined part.

5. What did you <u>think, Karen</u> of the movie?

   A think Karen

   B think, Karen,

   C think Karen,

   D Correct as it is

6. Tucked in a corner of the <u>garden, a small bench</u> offered rest.

   F garden a small bench

   G garden a small bench,

   H garden, a small bench,

   J Correct as it is

7. <u>Yes, it's true, Ed</u> that the meeting is today.

   A Yes it's true, Ed

   B Yes, it's true Ed,

   C Yes, it's true, Ed,

   D Correct as it is

8. Did you speak <u>to anyone, Nancy</u> about the promotion?

   F to anyone Nancy,

   G to anyone, Nancy,

   H to, anyone, Nancy,

   J Correct as it is

End Marks

Use a **period** at the end of a statement or a command.

> Sunshine filled the room. Hand me that wrench.

Use a **question mark** at the end of a question.

> What time does the library open?

Use an **exclamation point** at the end of a sentence that expresses excitement or strong feeling.

> What a close race!   Call for help!

Commas

Use commas to separate independent clauses in a **compound sentence.** Place a comma before the word that connects the clauses. Connecting words include *and*, *or*, *nor*, *but*, or *for*.

> Ted sells cars, and his brother repairs them.

Use commas to separate words or phrases that are written in a **series** of three or more. A series with a connecting word between every pair of items does not need commas.

> Jason, Doug, and Damon played golf on Monday.
>
> Amos likes to hike, to lift weights, and to watch TV.
>
> Order tuna or cheese or egg salad for me.

Use a comma to separate **introductory words** like *yes* or *no* from the rest of a sentence. Also use a comma to set off a **long phrase** that begins a sentence. Use a comma after short phrases of four words or less that begin sentences if it makes the **meaning clearer.**

> Yes, this is the right building.
>
> During the long flight, Marnie spent the time reading.
>
> Feeling tired, Elaine went to bed early.

Use a comma to set off the name of a person or thing **being spoken to** in a sentence.

> How was the trip, Marian?
>
> Paul, please sit down.
>
> Is it true, Mr. Grimes, that you are retiring?

Assessment

Read the following paragraphs and look at their numbered, underlined parts. Decide which punctuation mark is needed for each underlined part.

(1)   All around the <u>world</u> people share a love of music. They play the chin
(2) in China, the sansa in Africa, <u>and the oud</u> in the Middle East. What is the
(3) favorite instrument in <u>America.</u> Perhaps it is the guitar.

1. A world.

    B world?

    C world,

    D Correct as it is

2. F and the oud,

    G and, the oud

    H and, the oud,

    J Correct as it is

3. A America?

    B America!

    C America,

    D Correct as it is

(4)   To make a tasty <u>salad</u> start with fresh spinach. Add bean sprouts,
(5) water chestnuts, <u>onions and</u> bacon bits. Pour on your favorite
(6) dressing. <u>Toss, or shake</u> until everything is mixed. Dig in
(7) and <u>enjoy</u>

4. F salad,

    G salad.

    H salad!

    J Correct as it is

5. A onion and,

    B onions, and

    C onions, and,

    D Correct as it is

6. F Toss, or, shake

    G Toss or shake,

    H Toss or shake

    J Correct as it is

7. A enjoy?

    B enjoy,

    C enjoy!

    D Correct as it is

(8)   Many men, <u>women and children</u> visit the Grand Canyon.

(9)   They admire the <u>view, and</u> take pictures of the colorful rocks.

(10)   <u>Yes</u> it's a scenic wonder.

8. **F** women, and children

    G women and children,

    H women, and, children

    J Correct as it is

9. **A** view and

    B view and,

    C view, and,

    D Correct as it is

10. **F** Yes!

    G Yes,

    H Yes.

    J Correct as it is

Decide which end mark, if any, is needed in each sentence.

11. My checkbook is missing

    A ?   **B** ,   **C** !   **D** None

12. Is this the road to Fortune Bridge

    F .   **G** ?   **H** !   **J** None

13. Please form a line in the back of the room

    A .   **B** !   **C** ?   **D** None

14. How soon must you leave, ma'am

    F .   **G** ?   **H** ,   **J** None

15. Your research, Dr. Barnes, is well done

    A ?   **B** !   **C** .   **D** None

For each item, choose the sentence that has correct punctuation.

16. F Chad have you found your dog yet?

    G As hard as they tried the rangers could not put out the forest fire.

    H No the doctor is not in today.

    J Should the kitchen be painted white or blue or yellow?

17. A Joe brought the ribs and Heather made the salad.

    B Peach, vanilla, and lemon are my favorite flavorings.

    C Linda your room is a mess.

    D Did you shovel the snow!

18. F Yes Lily has moved to Maine.

    G Tony, and Dan joined the Navy.

    H By morning the rain had stopped.

    J Why is the flight delayed.

19. A No, Keith your wife isn't here.

    B Either rabbits, or squirrels ate the plants in the garden.

    C The road is too muddy for cars and it is not safe for bikes.

    D Panting heavily, the dog sat down in the shade.

20. F Help me move the couch, Ed.

    G Today is cool but, tomorrow should be warmer.

    H Yes sir the plums are fresh.

    J Dallas, and Atlanta have large airports.

21. A Neither flowers, nor grass grows in my yard.

    B Sarah, it's good to see you!

    C I'll have my hot dog with chili, and mustard.

    D Where will the convention be held this year.

22. F Tony address the envelopes, and mail them before Tuesday.

    G It's time to leave, for the mall is closing.

    H After dinner, we went for a walk.

    J Monday, Tuesday, and Wednesday, are the best days to visit Aunt Mae.

23. A As a matter of fact, Leslie, I like that song.

    B No, Mr. Richards, is not on duty now.

    C Do your homework first Dot and then watch TV.

    D Two deer jumped the fence, and munched on a tree.

Direct and Indirect Quotations

A **direct quotation** repeats the exact words of a speaker. When you write direct quotations, enclose them in quotation marks " ". Include the end mark for the quotation within the quotation marks. Other words in the sentence may identify the speaker. Do not put quotation marks around these words. Capitalize the first word of a direct quotation.

> The passenger asked, **"When will we get to Oak Street?"**
>
> The bus driver answered, **"Oak Street was the last stop."**
>
> **"I missed my stop!"** the passenger cried.

Indirect quotations summarize a speaker's message. They do not use the speaker's exact words. Do not enclose indirect quotations in quotation marks.

> **Indirect:**   Julie said that the rain was letting up.
>
> **Direct:**   Julie said, "The rain is letting up."

Read each sentence. If it includes a direct quotation, add quotation marks where they are needed. If it includes an indirect quotation, write *Indirect* on the line.

1. The coach shouted, Line up along the fence! _____

2. Twice this morning, Paul told me that he would be late for dinner.

   _____

3. Will this be on your credit card? asked the clerk. _____

4. Patrick Henry bravely said, Give me liberty, or give me death.

   _____

5. Who just rang the bell? asked Naomi. _____

6. Farmers are saying that it will be a good year for peaches.

   _____

7. The reviewer said that we should avoid this movie. _____

8. After she fell, the toddler cried, I want my mama! _____

9. The librarian told us that loud talking was not allowed. _____

B Practice

Rewrite the following direct quotations as indirect quotations.

1. Kyle asked, "What's the score?"

   _____

2. The pilot announced, "We will land in about twenty minutes."

   _____

3. "My sunburn really hurts!" complained Nicole.

   _____

Rewrite the following indirect quotations as direct quotations by completing each sentence.

4. The ranger said that we should boil our water before drinking it.

   The ranger said, _____

5. The weather forecaster said that today will be sunny.

   The weather forecaster said, _____

6. The guard at the door asked if we were members.

   The guard at the door asked, _____

For each item, circle the letter of the sentence that is capitalized and punctuated correctly.

7. A Lynn asked, "May I use your suntan lotion?"

   B Lynn asked, "may I use your suntan lotion?"

8. A The poet said that she had grown up in Alaska.

   B "The poet said" that she had grown up in Alaska.

9. A "Watch out for the runaway train"! screamed a man in the crowd.

   B "Watch out for the runaway train!" screamed a man in the crowd.

10. A Jessie told the vendor, "Chocolate is my favorite flavor."

    B "Jessie told the vendor," Chocolate is my favorite flavor.

C ◆ Apply

Read each sentence. If it is a direct quotation, rewrite it. Capitalize it correctly and add quotation marks wherever they are needed. If it is an indirect quotation, write *Indirect* on the line.

1. The nurse said, the doctor will see you now.

   _____

2. Britney complained that she couldn't see the screen.

   _____

3. Joshua suggested, let's get a cup of coffee and a piece of pie.

   _____

4. The fire is out of control! shouted the cook.

   _____

5. The detective asked, when did you discover the jewels were missing?

   _____

6. That cashier said that her register was closed.

   _____

7. would you like to rent a video? asked Steve.

   _____

8. Katy pleaded, give me just one taste of your banana split!

   _____

9. The movie star told reporters that she was retiring.

   _____

10. Dave told me that he is allergic to cats.

    _____

For each item, choose the sentence that is written correctly.

1. **A** Marcy said, "That color looks great on you.

   B My neighbor asked, "is that your cat"?

   C Debbie said, "My boss is looking for a new secretary."

   D "The mayor announced" that the city was planning a summer festival.

2. **F** The teacher said that our son is a good student.

   G When does the next show start? asked Michael.

   H "This isn't as easy as it looks, explained Sandy.

   J Laura whispered, "is the baby asleep yet?"

3. **A** Melanie screamed, "I win"!

   B "When will we know the results?" asked the patient.

   C Gina asked "what we wanted for a snack."

   D "The guide explained," this painting was found in an attic in France.

4. **F** The young mother murmured, "go to sleep now."

   G Grandpa said "That he had visited Egypt many years ago."

   H "What is your phone number?" the police officer asked the lost child.

   J "Tim said, I want a puppy!"

Read each sentence and look at the underlined part. Choose the answer that is written correctly for the underlined part.

5. The waitress asked, <u>do</u> you want fries with that?"

   A "Do

   B "do

   C "Do"

   D Correct as it is

6. The coach <u>said that her</u> team had trained hard for the big game.

   F said "That her

   G said "that her

   H said that "Her

   J Correct as it is

7. <u>"Vote for Pat! chanted</u> the candidate's supporters.

   A "Vote for Pat! chanted"

   B "Vote for Pat!" chanted

   C Vote for Pat! chanted

   D Correct as it is

8. The clerk asked, "Do you need some help with <u>your bags"?</u>

   F your bags"?"

   G your bags?

   H your bags?"

   J Correct as it is

A ▶ Introduce

Using Commas with Quotations

A **direct quotation** repeats the exact words of a speaker. When you write a direct quotation, set it off from the rest of the sentence with a comma.

Sometimes words that identify the speaker come before the quotation. Place a comma after these words, before the quotation. The comma should be outside the quotation marks.

> Jan said happily, "Next Monday is a holiday."
>
> Carlos asked, "What will you do on your day off?"

A quoted statement at the beginning of a sentence is followed by a comma, not a period. This comma is placed inside the quotation marks. Quoted questions and exclamations are followed by question marks and exclamation points, as usual. These end marks are also placed inside the quotation marks.

> "I'm going to the beach," said Jan.
>
> "Can I come along?" asked Carlos.
>
> "What a fine idea!" Jan replied.

For each sentence, add commas wherever they are needed.

1. The repairman said "This will cost about fifty dollars."

2. "Put your bags in the overhead bin" said the attendant.

3. "I saw a good movie last night" reported Mia.

4. Hector shouted "Slide!"

5. "My car is making a funny noise" said Grace.

6. Kristen complained "That was a really bad pun!"

7. The rules clearly state "The game ends when one player earns 100 points."

8. "Roses need plenty of sunlight and water" said Mrs. White.

9. Paul moaned "My house needs painting again!"

10. Justin said "Let's find a seat near the stage."

11. "We will be there in time for the next movie" said Julio.

B Practice

In the following sentences, explanatory words come before quoted words. Rewrite each sentence so that the explanatory words come after the quoted words. Be sure to use commas correctly.

> Example: The emcee said, "Tell us about yourself."
> "Tell us about yourself," said the emcee.

1. Lucia said, "That movie got good reviews."

   _____

2. The driver explained, "The brakes on my car failed."

   _____

3. The clerk said, "Your total is ten dollars."

   _____

In the following sentences, explanatory words follow quoted words. Rewrite each sentence so that the explanatory words come before the quoted words. Be sure to use commas correctly.

> Example: "Your flight has been delayed," said my aunt.
> My aunt said, "Your flight has been delayed."

4. "Save me a seat," said Andy.

   _____

5. "The baby just went to sleep," whispered Alicia.

   _____

6. "Always wear sunscreen," Heather's aunt said.

   _____

Read each pair of sentences. Circle the letter of the sentence in each pair in which commas are used correctly.

7. **A** Dan, said "I woke up early this morning,"

   B Dan said, "I woke up early this morning."

8. **A** "I'll see you to the door," Mr. Jackson said as he rose.

   B "I'll see you to the door." Mr. Jackson said, as he rose.

C Apply

Read each sentence. If commas have been used correctly, write *Correct* on the line. If commas have been omitted or used incorrectly, rewrite the sentence correctly on the line.

1. "I hope I get this job" said Julie.

   _____

2. Sonya asked "Will you need a packed lunch today?"

   _____

3. The doctor told Eric, "Eat more fiber and less fat."

   _____

4. The governor announced ",The budget is in good shape."

   _____

5. "My house has been for sale for six months" Bill told, his friend.

   _____

6. "Sun activity can affect our radios here on Earth," explained the scientist.

   _____

7. "Watch what I do" said the dance teacher.

   _____

8. Luis said "I'm looking for a good used car,"

   _____

9. "I'll answer the phone during lunch hour", Gina told her coworkers.

   _____

10. "Cloth from Africa is often brightly colored," replied the weaver.

   _____

D Check Up

For each item, choose the sentence that is punctuated correctly.

1. **A** "Our picnic is ruined", complained Rose.

   B "When will this rain end," asked the TV anchor.

   C Lila said, "It has been raining for days."

   D "The sun will come out soon" Ted promised.

2. **F** "Playing with model trains is fun", Brian told his son.

   G The nurse said, "I'll take your blood pressure."

   H "We always do things her way" muttered the angry employee.

   J "You are all suspects," ,the detective said.

3. **A** The author asked "To whom should I write the note?"

   B "We won the game" the announcer shouted.

   C "My cat likes living in our apartment", said Lisa.

   D The builder assured them, "We will begin your home this summer."

4. **F** "I'd say the party was a success," said the host.

   G "We need a new coach to help us." said the players.

   H The judge warned "I will not stand for another outburst".

   J Adam reminded his son "Water the flowers every other day,"

Read each sentence and look at the underlined part. Choose the answer that is written correctly for the underlined words and punctuation.

5. <u>Dale asked "What's</u> the score?"

   A Dale asked, "What's

   B Dale, asked "What's

   C Dale, asked, "What's

   D Correct as it is

6. "I have to work late <u>again,"</u> <u>complained Sam.</u>

   F again" complained Sam.

   G again", complained Sam.

   H again" complained, Sam.

   J Correct as it is

7. "We're having chicken <u>for dinner</u> <u>tonight" Lacey told</u> her family.

   A for dinner tonight", Lacey told

   B for dinner tonight," Lacey told

   C for dinner tonight" Lacey told,

   D Correct as it is

8. "How old is your little <u>boy,"</u> <u>asked the crossing guard.</u>

   F boy" asked the crossing guard.

   G boy", asked the crossing guard.

   H boy?" asked the crossing guard.

   J Correct as it is

Contractions

In a **contraction**, two words are combined. An apostrophe replaces one or more letters in the words. Many times, contractions are formed by combining a helping verb and the word *not*. The apostrophe replaces the *o* or the *no* in *not*.

can + not = can't	have + not = haven't
could + not = couldn't	was + not = wasn't
did + not = didn't	were + not = weren't
do + not = don't	should + not = shouldn't
has + not = hasn't	would + not = wouldn't

The following type of contraction is unusual because the *o* or the *no* in *not* isn't replaced. The spelling is changed when *will not* becomes a contraction.

will + not = won't

Other contractions combine a pronoun and a verb or helping verb. The apostrophe replaces part of the verb or helping verb.

he + is = he's	they + are = they're	it + is = it's	we + are = we're
she + is = she's	we + will = we'll	I + am = I'm	you + will = you'll
I + would = I'd	who + is = who's		

Do not confuse *it's* and *its*. *It's* means *it is*. The pronoun *its*, without an apostrophe, shows ownership.

It's time to go home. (*It is* time to go home.)

The dog chased its tail. (*Its* shows ownership of the tail.)

Write the two words that have been combined to make each contraction.

1. didn't = _____ + _____   6. they're = _____ + _____

2. he's = _____ + _____   7. you'll = _____ + _____

3. shouldn't = _____ + _____   8. she'll = _____ + _____

4. we'll = _____ + _____   9. wasn't = _____ + _____

5. I'm = _____ + _____   10. won't = _____ + _____

Write the contraction for each pair of words.

11. can + not = _____   14. is + not = _____

12. have + not = _____   15. will + not = _____

13. were + not = _____   16. we + are = _____

B Practice

For each item, circle the letter of the sentence in which the contraction is written correctly.

1. **A** It's almost quitting time.

    B Its' almost quitting time.

2. **A** We hope youll' sing at our wedding.

    B We hope you'll sing at our wedding.

3. **A** Didn't I see you at the mall yesterday?

    B Did'nt I see you at the mall yesterday?

4. **A** When wer'e in town, we'll stop by.

    B When we're in town, we'll stop by.

Rewrite each sentence using all possible contractions.

5. Laura could not recall the important phone number.

    _____

6. We will take a break at 10 A.M.

    _____

7. We are glad that you came.

    _____

8. It is not like him to be so late.

    _____

9. I would like to join you, but I cannot.

    _____

10. I am sure that you will be pleased with the results.

    _____

C Apply

Read each question. Then answer the question in a complete sentence. Be sure to use at least one contraction in your answer.

1. Q: Are you sure you know all the words to the national anthem?

   A: _____

2. Q: What movie are you going to see this weekend?

   A: _____

3. Q: What will we do if it rains on Saturday?

   A: _____

4. Q: Will the children order liver and onions at the restaurant?

   A: _____

5. Q: Is she coming to your birthday party?

   A: _____

6. Q: Which slice of pizza would you like?

   A: _____

7. Q: What would you do if you won one million dollars?

   A: _____

8. Q: How old will you be in 2023?

   A: _____

9. Q: Will the police officer give me a warning this time?

   A: _____

10. Q: Would you like popcorn plain or with butter?

    A: _____

D Check Up

For each item, choose the sentence in which the contraction is written correctly.

1. **A** I can't believe I won!

   B Aunt Beth said shel'l be visiting us this summer.

   C Did'nt you turn the lights off when you left the room?

   D If hes' late, I know that we will miss our flight.

2. **F** Theyr'e moving into their new house next month.

   G Who's the author of *Crime and Punishment?*

   H Im' sure that those shoes are going on sale soon.

   J Wel'l probably never know exactly what happened to Amelia Earhart.

3. **A** Wer'e eager to hear about your trip to Alaska.

   B Do'nt count your chickens before they hatch.

   C Weren't you the couple who wanted to rent this apartment?

   D I guess its not my concern.

4. **F** Kim willn't have enough money to buy a house for at least another year.

   G Shouldn't' you be mowing the lawn today?

   H Pardon me, but have'nt we met before?

   J Alex says he won't take a trip this summer after all.

Read each sentence and look at the underlined word. Choose the answer that is written correctly for the underlined word.

5. We <u>werenl'</u> able to get four tickets to the concert.

   A were'n't

   B weren't

   C were'nt

   D Correct as it is

6. If <u>its</u> sunny tomorrow, we'll have a picnic.

   F it's

   G i'ts

   H its'

   J Correct as it is

7. <u>I'll</u> never forget your kindness when I needed help.

   A Il'l

   B Ill'

   C I'l'l

   D Correct as it is

8. Shelly <u>has'nt</u> come to work in over a week.

   F hasnt'

   G hasn't'

   H hasn't

   J Correct as it is

Possessive Nouns

A **possessive noun** shows ownership of the noun that follows it.

> <u>Sylvia's</u> son is in first grade. (*Sylvia's* is a possessive noun. The son belongs to Sylvia.)

To make the possessive form of a singular noun, add an apostrophe followed by the letter *s*. Follow this rule even when the singular noun ends in *s*.

> Marcy**'s** eyes   Barb**'s** job   James**'s** father

To make the possessive form of a plural noun that ends in *s*, simply add an apostrophe.

> the Jacksons**'** dog   the counselors**'** offices

Some plural nouns do not end in *s*. To make one of these nouns show possession, treat it the same as a singular noun. That is, add an apostrophe followed by an *s*.

> men**'s** cologne   women**'s** coats

Circle the possessive noun in each sentence. Indicate on the line whether it is singular or plural. Write *S* for singular or *P* for plural.

1. _____ We still need Laura's signature on the birthday card.

2. _____ The tennis pro says that Isaiah's backhand needs work.

3. _____ Those squirrels' tails are really bushy.

4. _____ I'm afraid those flowers' petals have all fallen off.

5. _____ Can you see the artist's name at the bottom of the painting?

6. _____ The Mitchells were invited to sit at the captain's table.

7. _____ My sisters' voices sound alike.

8. _____ Owen caught the driver's eye and signaled her to slow down.

9. _____ Two women's clubs meet in this room.

10. _____ Kristen asked for two more doctors' opinions.

B Practice

For each item, circle the letter of the sentence in which the possessive noun is written correctly.

1. **A** The three robbers stories were all different.

   B The three robbers' stories were all different.

2. **A** My dogs bark scared the delivery man.

   B My dog's bark scared the delivery man.

3. **A** The parents were proud of their children's artwork.

   B The parents were proud of their childrens' artwork.

4. **A** Charles's' car is parked in a no-parking zone.

   B Charles's car is parked in a no-parking zone.

5. **A** Because I trusted her, I took the guide's advice

   B Because I trusted her, I took the guides' advice.

Rewrite each phrase using a possessive noun.

> **Example:** the uniforms that belong to those players
> those players' uniforms

6. the station that belongs to that nurse _____

7. windows that belong to the tellers _____

8. the tools that belong to the plumber _____

9. the rights of the voters _____

10. the footprints of the robbers _____

11. the league of the men _____

12. games that belong to the children _____

13. a fortune that belongs to a princess _____

14. the orders of the king _____

Each sentence below has one possessive noun. If the possessive noun is written correctly, write *Correct* on the line. If the possessive noun is not written correctly, rewrite it correctly on the line.

1. Kristen read the builders plan and asked him questions.

    _____

2. Lee's brownies were a big hit at the picnic.

    _____

3. While its owner was away, Mickey waved the sorcerers' wand.

    _____

4. The patient's wheelchairs are ready for them.

    _____

5. She gave good service, so make this waitress' tip fair.

    _____

6. Those directors are good at making childrens movies.

    _____

7. The minister's sermons show that he works hard on them.

    _____

8. The get-well card came from the foremans' coworkers.

    _____

9. Have you seen the Bakers new backyard deck?

    _____

10. In some households, it is the mans' duty to take out the trash.

    _____

11. Hang your food out of the bears reach, or they will eat it.

    _____

D Check Up

For each item, choose the sentence in which the possessive noun is written correctly.

1. **A** Sonyas' car wouldn't start this morning.

   B The toddlers' moms watched their children and caught up on news.

   C I lost my babysitters phone number, but I finally found it.

   D Bostons' downtown is exciting and historic.

2. **F** The players scores were hidden from them until the last round.

   G Everyone at the party wanted one of Chris' cookies.

   H Teresa's sister is visiting her next weekend.

   J The Smiths home is getting too small for them.

3. **A** Sometimes Miles's temper gets the better of him.

   B To make quiche, follow this chefs directions exactly.

   C The two brother's project kept them busy for weeks.

   D This may be Douglas' last chance to prove himself.

4. **F** Denice can cut either mens' or womens' hair.

   G The swimmers expressions showed their desire to win.

   H Michaels jokes always make his friends laugh.

   J I believe that the children's safety is our most important concern.

Read each sentence and look at the underlined word. Choose the answer that is written correctly for the underlined word.

5. The <u>speakers</u> voice was so soft we could barely hear it.

   A speakers'

   B speaker's

   C Correct as it is

6. Please hand me the <u>babys'</u> bottle. She seems hungry.

   F babies'

   G baby's

   H Correct as it is

7. Make a list of your <u>relative's</u> addresses to add to the guest list.

   A relatives'

   B relatives's

   C Correct as it is

8. <u>Tess's</u> garden is filled with roses and daisies.

   F Tess'

   G Tess's'

   H Correct as it is

Letter Parts

A business letter has these six parts.

Heading: The date the letter is written. Be sure to insert a comma between the day of the month and the year.

Inside Address: The receiver's address. It has three lines: the name of the business or person; the street address; and the city, state, and ZIP code. Capitalize all important words in the business name. Capitalize the names of the street, the city, and the state. Insert a comma between the name of the city and the name of the state.

Greeting: The letter's "hello." Capitalize each important word in the greeting. Place a colon after the last word.

Body: The message. Indent the first word of each paragraph.

Closing: The letter's "good-bye." Capitalize the first word but not the second. Place a comma after the closing.

Signature and Name: Sign your name below the closing. Print or type your name below your signature.

(Heading)	May 3, 2004
(Inside Address)	Acme Sign Company 146 Maple Street Durham, North Carolina 27701
(Greeting)	Dear Sir or Madam:
(Body)	Please send me a catalog of your signs.
(Closing)	Yours truly,
(Signature)	*Leah Selden*
(Name)	Leah Selden

Each letter part below contains one or more errors. Rewrite each part correctly.

1. 386 march avenue _____

2. sincerely Yours, _____

3. Dear sir or madam! _____

4. april, 8 2004 _____

The names, addresses, phrases, and dates below are from a letter. They are out of order. Some have capitalization or punctuation errors. Decide where each one belongs. Write it correctly in its proper place in the letter form at the bottom of the page.

What-a-Buy Appliances	Tiera King
Respectfully Yours:	213 Oak street
Tiera King	september, 6 2003
Livermore California, 94550	Dear sir or madam,

     I am writing in response to your ad for a sales clerk in your store. I am very familiar with the video and audio equipment you sell. Please send me an application for the job.

                                        _____

_____

_____

_____

_____

_____

_____

_____

_____

                                        _____

                                        _____

                                        _____

Apply

Use the following information to write a business letter on the lines below. Give the letter today's date. Write a letter of complaint about a pair of shoes that you bought from City Streets Outfitters, 4167 Urban Avenue, Chicago, Illinois 60601. Be sure to capitalize and punctuate the letter correctly.

_____

_____

_____

_____

_____

_____

_____

_____

_____

_____

_____

_____

_____

_____

◆ D Check Up

Read the following letter and pay special attention to the underlined parts. Choose the answer that is written correctly for each underlined part.

(1) <u>January 21 2004</u>

Goodtime Cruises

(2) <u>17649 Jordan drive</u>

(3) <u>New York, New York 10003</u>

(4) <u>Dear sir or Madam:</u>

I would like to learn more about your cruises. My wife and I are planning a vacation in March of 2005. Please send us a brochure that describes your cruises and gives their prices. Thank you very much.

(5) <u>Yours Truly,</u>

John Hsu

John Hsu

1. **A** january 21 2004

   B January 21, 2004

   C January, 21 2004

   D Correct as it is

2. **F** 17649 jordan drive

   G 17649 Jordan Drive,

   H 17649 Jordan Drive

   J Correct as it is

3. **A** New york, New York 10003

   B new york, New York 10003

   C New York New York 10003

   D Correct as it is

4. **F** Dear Sir or Madam:

   G Dear Sir or Madam,

   H Dear Sir Or Madam:

   J Correct as it is

5. **A** Yours Truly

   B Yours truly,

   C Yours truly:

   D Correct as it is

Review

Quotations

A **direct quotation** repeats the exact words of a speaker. Write a direct quotation within quotation marks and set it off from the rest of the sentence with a comma. Write the end mark for the quotation within the quotation marks. Capitalize the first word of the quotation.

> **Direct:** The clerk asked, "Do you need a gift box?"
>
> "I would like a gift box," I replied.

An **indirect quotation** does not use a speaker's exact words. Do not enclose it in quotation marks or set it off with a comma.

> **Indirect:** The clerk asked if I needed a gift box.

Contractions

A **contraction** combines two words. An apostrophe replaces one or more letters.

> would + not = wouldn't   we + will = we'll

Possessive Nouns

A **possessive noun** shows ownership.

> **Singular:** Add an apostrophe and *s*. (a *lawyer's* briefcase)
>
> **Plural ending in** *s*: Add an apostrophe. (the *birds'* cries)
>
> **Plural not ending in** *s*: Add an apostrophe and *s*. (*men's* hats)

Letter Parts

A business letter follows a special form and has six parts.

(Heading)	April 20, 2004
(Inside Address)	Best Computer 275 Crane Avenue Jonesboro, Arkansas 72401
(Greeting)	Dear Sir or Madam:
(Body)	Please send me a catalog of computers for sale.
(Closing)	Sincerely yours,
(Signature)	*Seth Morgan*
(Name)	Seth Morgan

For each item, choose the sentence that is written correctly.

1. A Julia said "Let's take a long walk."

    B "Our customers' names are in a database," explained the manager.

    C Imani warned "The mall closes in fifteen minutes,"

    D The operator asked, "what number are you calling?"

2. F "Will this be on the test" asked the students?

    G "Save my place." said Sean.

    H "Look out below!" shouted the house painter.

    J Malik muttered, "This seems like a lot of work".

3. A Its' past my bedtime.

    B "Ca'nt we forget the past and start over?" Cheryl pleaded.

    C I'm not used to wearing glasses yet.

    D The bus doesnt' stop here.

4. F The general said that it was time to attack.

    G "The mayor said, This has been a great day for the city."

    H The librarian told us that "the book had been ordered."

    J "The car keys are on the dresser, said Tony as he went out the door.

5. A Paris' dream is to one day run her own business.

    B That was the night managers' job but he forgot to do it.

    C When are these childrens' parents coming back?

    D Meet us at the Pruitts' house.

6. F "Run for your lives"! shouted the frightened woman.

    G Ashlee asked, "Who put this paper on my desk?"

    H The hostess said, "Come this way".

    J "All visitors must wear a badge" said the sign at the door.

7. A I'd never heard that singer before.

    B Wont' you come to my party?

    C The driver said that he had'nt seen the stop sign.

    D Wer'e making progress now.

8. F Marcus' brother has a new job.

    G Hang the guest's coats in this closet until the party ends.

    H It is each customers' right to expect good service.

    J My boss's husband sent her roses.

Read the letter below and look at its underlined parts. Choose the answer that is written correctly for each underlined part.

(9)   <u>august 9, 2003</u>

Model Madness
(10)   <u>1358 hall street</u>
(11)   <u>Battle Creek Michigan 49016</u>

(12)   <u>Dear Sir or Madam,</u>

(13)   I am looking for model ship kits that I can make with my <u>son's</u>. They are seven and nine years old. Pete and Matt are interested in battleships and subs from the World War II era. Please send me a current catalog.

(14)   <u>Yours truly</u>

Megan Ingram

Megan Ingram

9. A August 9, 2003
    B August, 9 2003
    C august, 9 2003
    D Correct as it is

10. F 1358 Hall street
    G 1358 hall Street
    H 1358 Hall Street
    J Correct as it is

11. A Battle Creek, Michigan, 49016
    B Battle Creek, Michigan 49016
    C Battle creek Michigan 49016
    D Correct as it is

12. F Dear Sir or Madam:
    G Dear sir or madam,
    H Dear Sir Or Madam:
    J Correct as it is

13. A son's'
    B sons'
    C sons
    D Correct as it is

14. F Yours Truly
    G Yours truly,
    H Yours Truly:
    J Correct as it is

Read the letter below and look at its underlined parts. Choose the answer that is written correctly for each underlined part.

(15) October 21, 2004

Vision Luggage Company

(16) 2646 Elm street
Dallas, Texas 75225

(17) Dear sir or madam:

I am writing about a problem I had with a Vision suitcase. I used it only once. Even though I was careful, the zipper broke. I am asking that you refund my money or send me a new suitcase.

(18) Respectfully Yours,

Jason Ward

Jason Ward

15. A october 21, 2004

  B October, 21 2004

  C October 21 2004

  D Correct as it is

16. F 2646 Elm street

  G 2646 elm Street

  H 2646 Elm Street

  J Correct as it is

17. A Dear sir or madam,

  B Dear Sir or Madam:

  C Dear Sir or Madam,

  D Correct as it is

18. F Respectfully yours,

  G respectfully yours,

  H respectfully Yours,

  J Correct as it is

Read the paragraph below and look at its underlined parts. Choose the answer that is written correctly for each underlined part.

(19) If you're like most Americans, youl'l be eating out soon. Most people's schedules are busy today. You and I know that it's tempting to order a pizza instead of cooking at home. But be
(20) careful. You ca'n't control your diet easily when you eat out.

19. A you'll

  B youll'

  C youll

  D Correct as it is

20. F ca'nt

  G cant'

  H can't

  J Correct as it is

Posttest

Decide which punctuation mark, if any, should be added to each sentence.

1. "Do you know how to run this machine? asked Ben.

   A .   **B** ,   **C** "   **D** None

2. Has the rain stopped yet

   F ,   **G** ?   **H** '   **J** None

3. "Remember to sign your check," said Grace.

   A .   **B** '   **C** ?   **D** None

4. Answer the phone Melissa.

   F ,   **G** ?   **H** "   **J** None

5. Wouldnt you like another cookie before you go?

   A '   **B** ,   **C** !   **D** None

Choose the word or phrase that best completes each sentence.

6. Which walks _____, a turtle or a snail?

   F more slower

   G more slowly

   H most slowliest

   J most slowly

7. The main roads and the bridge _____ snow-covered and slippery.

   A is

   B are

   C was

   D has been

8. The phone rang several times, but no one _____ it.

   F has answer

   G answer

   H was answered

   J answered

9. Each morning I walk the dog and _____ the goldfish.

   A fed

   B will feed

   C feed

   D has fed

For each item, choose the sentence that is written properly and has correct capitalization and punctuation. Be sure the sentence you choose is complete.

10. **F** "I love Japanese art," said Jill.

    G what is the score?

    H that cereal is on sale this week.

    J "pick any card," said the magician.

11. **A** Sat by the side of the road.

    B Running down the hill at top speed.

    C A little boy flying a blue kite.

    D The work crew is mowing the lawn.

12. **F** Give me a refill my coffee is cold.

    G I can't believe it, I won the lottery!

    H Today's crossword puzzle is easy.

    J Let Ray open the jar, he is strong.

13. **A** This Halloween, Cheryl is going to two parties.

    B The Smith family took an Elevator to the top of the Empire State Building.

    C Cal planted a european beech tree in his Back Yard.

    D Are you inviting dr. Vargo and her Husband?

14. **F** My uncle lost his job, but she got a new one quickly.

    G Timmy caught a turtle and put it in an aquarium.

    H Noah blames themselves for the accident.

    J The girl which wanted mint ice cream got chocolate by mistake.

15. **A** Give your application to he.

    B Is this bike yours or mine?

    C Can you ask yours brother for a lift to the garage?

    D Leave them dirty boots outside the door.

16. **F** I could hardly wait to get home.

    G Sean can't hardly reach the shelf.

    H Tina hasn't never ridden in a plane.

    J Don't let no one into the store.

17. **A** The worker's paychecks must be sent to them today.

    B The knight knelt before the kings' throne and told him the news.

    C Where can I find children's books?

    D Kris' handwriting is messy.

Read each pair of underlined sentences. Then choose the sentence that best combines those two sentences.

18. Jed likes country music.
    Andy likes country music.

    F The music that Andy and Jed like is country.

    G Andy likes country music, so Jed does, too.

    H Jed likes country music, so does Andy.

    J Jed and Andy like country music.

19. Maria watched a late-night movie.
    The movie was scary.

    A The movie that Maria thought was scary came on late at night.

    B Maria watched a scary, late-night movie.

    C The movie that Maria watched was a late-night movie, and it was scary.

    D Maria watched a movie that was scary, and the scary movie came on late at night.

20. Anna turned on her bedroom television.
    Anna flipped through the channels.

    F The television in Anna's bedroom was turned on by her, and she also flipped through the channels.

    G In her bedroom, Anna flipped through the channels of the television that was also in her bedroom.

    H Anna turned on her bedroom television and flipped through the channels.

    J Anna turned on her bedroom television, and Anna flipped through the channels, too.

21. The baby was happy.
    The baby had just been fed.

    A The baby was happy and had just been fed, too.

    B The baby had just been happy and fed.

    C The happy baby had just been fed.

    D The baby was happy, and the baby had just been fed.

Read each paragraph. Then choose the sentence that best fills the blank.

22. _____. Never leave food out. Store all foods in a bear-proof container. Don't bring anything that smells like food into your tent at night. You don't want to get between a hungry bear and its next meal.

    F Bears in the wild can be dangerous.

    G Be extra careful with food when you camp in bear country.

    H Camping is fun.

    J Choose the foods for a camping trip carefully.

23. After the play, the audience clapped for five minutes. They even stood and cheered for the cast. The next day, critics praised the play in their reviews. _____.

    A I have a ticket to tonight's play.

    B My sister has a role in the latest hit play.

    C Many people enjoy plays.

    D Clearly, the play was a big success.

24. The salesman was taught to follow these steps. First, introduce yourself to the customer. Next, tell him or her what you are selling. _____. Finally, say how much the product costs and ask how many the customer wants.

    F Then ring the doorbell.

    G Then give the customer a receipt.

    H Then explain why the customer needs the product.

    J Then thank the customer for the sale.

25. Dee hosed all the dirt off her dusty car. Then she washed the car with soapy water. _____. Finally, she dried the car with soft rags. At last Dee's car was clean.

    A She washes her car every week.

    B Next, she rinsed the soap off.

    C Next, she drove her clean car to work.

    D Next, Dee waxed and buffed her car.

Read each topic sentence. Then choose the answer that best develops the topic sentence.

26. The Mustangs are likely to win the championship for two reasons.

   F   Fans are excited. They sense that victory is near.

   G   The Mustangs have not won it for a long time. They finished third last year.

   H   Ticket sales this year are above average. The ballpark is always full.

   J   The Mustang pitchers are the best in the league. The team's hitters have been coming through in the clutch.

27. Sara is always willing to try new foods.

   A   She recently dined on chocolate-covered ants. She has tried eating fish eggs and squid.

   B   Foods that one person thinks are strange may be normal for another. Likes and dislikes may depend on what foods you are used to.

   C   Some foods make her sick. She cannot eat bananas, for example.

   D   Some people eat worms and raw fish. Others stick to more normal foods.

28. It is clear that Matt needs a new sweatshirt.

   F   Matt almost always wears an old red cap. His friends make fun of it, but he doesn't care.

   G   His old sweatshirt is torn and stained. No amount of washing will make it smell fresh again.

   H   Matt's sweatshirt is gold and blue. The name of his favorite football team is printed on it.

   J   A new sweatshirt could cost $30. A really nice one might cost as much as $75.

Read each paragraph. Then choose the sentence that does <u>not</u> belong in the paragraph.

29.   1. Trees are useful in many ways. 2. Both oaks and maples grow on the streets of our town. 3. Trees provide wood for new houses. 4. Trees also give off oxygen and help clean the air.

A Sentence 1

B Sentence 2

C Sentence 3

D Sentence 4

30.   1. I took my nephew to the playground yesterday. 2. Playground equipment is often dangerous. 3. A child can fall from the top of a tall slide. 4. Swings can hit a passing child in the head.

F Sentence 1

G Sentence 2

H Sentence 3

J Sentence 4

31.   1. Today was a busy day at the shop. 2. It seemed like the phone would never stop ringing. 3. Customers kept asking questions and making demands. 4. My brother works at the shop, too.

A Sentence 1

B Sentence 2

C Sentence 3

D Sentence 4

32.   1. The Tuckers split up the Sunday paper, as usual. 2. Cal took the comics. 3. The Sunday paper costs two dollars. 4. Leslie took the front page.

F Sentence 1

G Sentence 2

H Sentence 3

J Sentence 4

Read the following paragraphs and look at their underlined parts. Choose the answer that is written correctly for each underlined part.

(33)   It hadn't rained for <u>weeks, the land</u> was dry and dusty.
(34) Precious topsoil <u>was lift</u> and blown through the air. None of the
(35) farmers could remember a <u>more drier</u> summer in years. Most of
(36) them <u>said that their</u> crops would surely be ruined if the weather
       didn't change soon.

33. **A** weeks the land

    B weeks. The land

    C weeks. the land

    D Correct as it is

35. **A** drier

    B more drily

    C most drily

    D Correct as it is

34. **F** lifts

    G lifting

    H was lifted

    J Correct as it is

36. **F** said that, "Their crops

    G said, "that their crops

    H said, "That their crops

    J Correct as it is

(37)   A new restaurant has opened on <u>Carroll Street?</u> This reporter
(38) <u>hasn't never</u> seen such excitement about a new restaurant before.
(39) Everyone is buzzing about the Thirsty Camel and <u>it's</u> menu. Diners
(40) are flocking to the place for fresh <u>soups, salads, and sandwiches.</u>

37. **A** Carroll Street,

    B Carroll Street.

    C Carroll Street

    D Correct as it is

39. **A** its

    B its'

    C it's'

    D Correct as it is

38. **F** didn't never

    G hasn't hardly ever

    H has never

    J Correct as it is

40. **F** soups, salads, and, sandwiches.

    G soups, salads and sandwiches.

    H soups salads and sandwiches.

    J Correct as it is

Read the following letter and look at its underlined parts. Choose the answer that is written correctly for each underlined part.

(41)   June 15 2003

Sun Safety
527 Redwood Road
(42) Phoenix, Arizona 85020

(43) Dear sir or madam:

(44)   I know that people often say, "I look better with a suntan." These people don't think about the damage the sun can do. As a lifeguard, I want to share that knowledge. Please send me a copy of your booklet **(45)** "safety in the sun." I will read it to my students.

(46)   Sincerely

Hal Meeker

Hal Meeker

41. **A** june 15 2003

  B June 15 2003,

  C June 15, 2003

  D Correct as it is

42. **F** Phoenix, Arizona, 85020

  G Phoenix Arizona 85020

  H phoenix, arizona 85020

  J Correct as it is

43. **A** Dear sir or madam,

  B Dear Sir or Madam:

  C Dear Sir or madam,

  D Correct as it is

44. **F** say, I look better

  G say "I look better

  H "say, I look better

  J Correct as it is

45. **A** "Safety in the sun."

  B "Safety In The Sun."

  C "Safety in the Sun."

  D Correct as it is

46. **F** sincerely

  G Sincerely,

  H Sincerely:

  J Correct as it is

Posttest Answer Key and Evaluation Chart

The Posttest checks your mastery of the language skills studied. Circle the question numbers that you answered incorrectly and review the practice pages covering those skills.

Key

1.	C	29.	B
2.	G	30.	F
3.	D	31.	D
4.	F	32.	H
5.	A	33.	B
6.	G	34.	H
7.	B	35.	A
8.	J	36.	J
9.	C	37.	B
10.	F	38.	H
11.	D	39.	A
12.	H	40.	J
13.	A	41.	C
14.	G	42.	J
15.	B	43.	B
16.	F	44.	J
17.	C	45.	C
18.	J	46.	G
19.	B		
20.	H		
21.	C		
22.	G		
23.	D		
24.	H		
25.	B		
26.	J		
27.	A		
28.	G		

Tested Skills	Question Numbers	Practice Pages
pronouns	15	23–26, 27–30
antecedent agreement	14	31–34
verbs	8, 9, 34	35–38, 39–42, 43–46
subject/verb agreement	7	47–50
adjectives and adverbs	6, 35	51–54, 55–58, 59–62
use of negatives	16, 38	63–66
sentence recognition	11, 12, 33	71–74, 75–78
sentence combining	18, 19, 20, 21	79–82, 83–86, 87–90, 91–94
topic sentences	22, 23	99–102, 103–106
supporting sentences	26, 27, 28	107–110, 111–114
sequence	24, 25	115–118, 119–122
unrelated sentences	29, 30, 31, 32	123–126
proper nouns and proper adjectives	13	131–134, 135–138
first words	10, 45	139–142
end marks	2, 37	147–150
commas	4, 40	151–154, 155–158, 159–162
quotations	1, 3, 36, 44	167–170, 171–174
apostrophes in contractions and possessives	5, 17, 39	175–178, 179–182
letter parts	41, 42, 43, 46	183–186

Answer Key

◆ **Unit 1 Usage**

◆ **Lesson 1 Nouns**

Page 18: 1. newspaper, door, **2.** Jack, football, college, **3.** Golden Gate Bridge, fog, **4.** pilot, plane, Detroit, **5.** Austin, capital, Texas, **6.** paintings, Georgia O'Keeffe, flowers, **7.** birdcalls, forest, **8.** George Washington, honesty, **9.** April, tulips, garden, **10.** members, team, game

Page 19: 1. P, **2.** P, **3.** S, **4.** P, **5.** S, **6.** S, **7.** P, **8.** S, **9.** P, **10.** P, **11.** Halloween, **12.** Correct, **13.** Eiffel Tower, Paris, France, **14.** New York Yankees, World Series, **15.** Atlantic Ocean

Page 20: Answers will vary.

Page 21: 1. A, **2.** F, **3.** C, **4.** F, **5.** C, **6.** H, **7.** B, **8.** J

◆ **Lesson 2 Personal Pronouns**

Page 22: 1. *Underline:* her; *Circle:* Iris, **2.** *Underline:* its; *Circle:* tree, **3.** *Underline:* he; *Circle:* Ken, **4.** *Underline:* you; *Circle:* Evie, **5.** *Underline:* she; *Circle:* Sharese, **6.** *Underline:* they; *Circle:* butterflies, **7.** *Underline:* yours; *Circle:* Brad, **8.** *Underline:* I; *Circle:* Jean

Page 23: 1. We, **2.** him, **3.** She, **4.** her, **5.** I, **6.** He, **7.** her, **8.** They, **9.** us, **10.** them, **11.** me, **12.** We, **13.** She, **14.** me, **15.** him

Page 24: 1. *Circle:* its; *arrow to:* spider, **2.** *Circle:* mine; *arrow to:* I, **3.** *Circle:* his; *arrow to:* Mr. Jackson, **4.** *Circle:* their; *arrow to:* fans, **5.** *Circle:* his; *arrow to:* actor, **6.** your, **7.** my, **8.** hers, **9.** their, **10.** her

Page 25: 1. A, **2.** J, **3.** B, **4.** F, **5.** B, **6.** H, **7.** D, **8.** G, **9.** D

◆ **Lesson 3 More Pronouns**

Page 26: 1. who, **2.** Whose, **3.** who, **4.** that, **5.** whom, **6.** who, **7.** whom, **8.** that, **9.** Who, **10.** which, **11.** who, **12.** that, **13.** Whose

Page 27: 1. *Underline:* herself; *Circle:* Barb, **2.** *Underline:* themselves; *Circle:* They, **3.** *Underline:* herself; *Circle:* queen, **4.** *Underline:* yourself; *Circle:* you, **5.** *Underline:* themselves; *Circle:* children,

6. *Underline:* myself; *Circle:* I, **7.** *Underline:* yourself; *Circle:* you, **8.** *Underline:* itself; *Circle:* dog, **9.** *Underline:* himself; *Circle:* artist, **10.** *Underline:* ourselves; *Circle:* We, **11.** himself, **12.** herself, **13.** themselves, **14.** myself

Page 28: 1. *Underline:* which; *Circle:* factory **2.** *Underline:* who; *Circle:* baker, **3.** *Underline:* that; *Circle:* door, **4.** *Underline:* herself; *Circle:* Emily, **5.** *Underline:* themselves; *Circle:* crew, **6.** *Underline:* himself; *Circle:* owner, **7.** *Underline:* myself; *Circle:* I, **8.** *Underline:* who; *Circle:* runner, **9.** *Underline:* whom; *Circle:* waiter, **10.** *Underline:* yourself; *Circle:* You

The people <u>who</u> boarded the Titanic were ready for a smooth trip. The captain <u>himself</u> was quite sure he would have a good cruise. But then the ship hit an iceberg. The ship, <u>which</u> was believed to be unsinkable, began to sink. People headed for the lifeboats, but <u>they</u> couldn't find enough boats for everyone. Many of the people were not able to save <u>themselves</u>. About 1,500 lives were lost.

Page 29: 1. C, **2.** F, **3.** A, **4.** G, **5.** B, **6.** J, **7.** D, **8.** G

◆ **Lesson 4 Antecedent Agreement**

Page 30: 1. *Underline:* their; *Circle:* soldiers, **2.** *Underline:* her; *Circle:* Inez, **3.** *Underline:* him; *Circle:* Uncle Bob, **4.** *Underline:* it; *Circle:* poem, **5.** *Underline:* he; *Circle:* Grandpa, **6.** *Underline:* their; *Circle:* knights, **7.** *Underline:* it; *Circle:* magazine, **8.** *Underline:* they; *Circle:* fighters, **9.** *Underline:* her; *Circle:* driver, **10.** *Underline:* his; *Circle:* artist

Page 31: 1. B, **2.** B, **3.** A, **4.** A, **5.** his; *Circle:* John, **6.** she; *Circle:* Liza, **7.** they; *Circle:* matches, **8.** who; *Circle:* toddler, **9.** his; *Circle:* prince, **10.** we; *Circle:* we

Page 32: 1. Correct, **2.** When I peel an onion, <u>my</u> eyes water. **3.** Correct, **4.** The judges looked at the dog carefully and gave <u>it</u> first prize. **5.** The author himself (*or* <u>herself</u>) came to the party. **6.** My daughter fell off

Answer Key *continued*

her bike, but <u>she</u> got right back on. **7.** Our pilot, <u>who</u> had flown many hours, brought us down safely. **8.** Michelle told <u>herself</u> to do her best. **9.** Pull these weeds because I hate seeing <u>them</u> in the garden. **10.** Correct

Page 33: 1. A, **2.** G, **3.** C, **4.** J, **5.** C, **6.** G, **7.** A, **8.** J

◆ Lesson 5 Verbs

Page 34: 1. <u>paid</u>, **2.** <u>carries</u>, <u>have sold</u>, **3.** <u>is</u>; *Write:* is, **4.** <u>have arrived</u>, **5.** <u>came</u>, <u>was</u>; *Write:* was, **6.** <u>should sew</u>, **7.** <u>must finish</u>, <u>can play</u>, **8.** <u>are</u>; *Write:* are

Page 35: *Regular:* act, jump, turn; *Irregular:* bring, drive, keep, ride, run

Page 36: 1. sewed, **2.** painted, **3.** elected, **4.** blew, **5.** annoyed, **6.** has taken, **7.** trained, **8.** has thrown, **9.** has seen, **10.** prepared

Page 37: 1. B, **2.** H, **3.** A, **4.** J, **5.** A, **6.** G, **7.** A, **8.** J

◆ Lesson 6 Verbs and Their Tenses

Page 38: 1. <u>ate</u>; Past, **2.** <u>will speak</u>; Future, **3.** <u>remembers</u>; Present, **4.** <u>will start</u>; Future, **5.** <u>earned</u>; Past, **6.** <u>attended</u>, <u>received</u>; Past, **7.** <u>understand</u>; Present, **8.** <u>fixed</u>; Past

Page 39: 1. B, **2.** G, **3.** D, **4.** G, **5.** B

Page 40: 1. fell, **2.** will enjoy, **3.** searched, **4.** plays, **5.** Listen, **6.** will repair, **7.** hurries, hurried, **8.** chops, chopped, **9.** will get, **10.** ends, **11.** sits, sat, **12.** shops, **13.** bought, **14.** will skate

Page 41: 1. A, **2.** F, **3.** C, **4.** J, **5.** C, **6.** F, **7.** C, **8.** G

◆ Lesson 7 Perfect Tenses of Verbs

Page 42: 1. <u>named, had served</u>; *Write:* had served, **2.** <u>have been</u>, <u>met</u>; *Write:* have been, **3.** <u>has</u>, <u>will have seen</u>; *Write:* will have seen, **4.** <u>has written</u>, <u>wants</u>; *Write:* has written, **5.** <u>had wandered, were found</u>; *Write:* had wandered, **6.** <u>sails</u>, <u>has</u>, <u>will have spent</u>; *Write:* will have spent

Page 43: 1. B, **2.** A, **3.** B, **4.** A, **5.** A, **6.** B, **7.** A, **8.** B, **9.** A, **10.** A

Page 44: 1. My sons have eaten the whole pizza. **2.** A mouse has lived in my wall for months. **3.** Next week, Gina will have biked to work five times. **4.** I did not know that you had wanted a ticket too. **5.** had typed, **6.** have coughed, **7.** will have eaten, **8.** will have saved, **9.** has run, **10.** had driven

Page 45: 1. B, **2.** G, **3.** D, **4.** F, **5.** A, **6.** G, **7.** D

◆ Lesson 8 Agreement of Subjects and Verbs

Page 46: 1. <u>son</u>, <u>sells</u>; S, **2.** <u>flowers</u>, <u>bloom</u>; P, **3.** <u>museum</u>, <u>opens</u>; S, **4.** <u>clubs</u>, <u>charge</u>; P, **5.** <u>I</u>, <u>am</u>; S, **6.** <u>forecasters</u>, <u>use</u>; P, **7.** <u>Crows</u>, <u>have</u>; P, **8.** <u>truck</u>, <u>carries</u>; S

Page 47: 1. *Circle:* temperature; *Draw line through:* on the islands; *Underline:* varies, **2.** *Circle:* kindergartners; *Draw line through:* after a short nap; *Underline:* have, **3.** *Circle:* Lawyers; *Draw line through:* for the defendant; *Underline:* present, **4.** *Circle:* leader; *Draw line through:* of the rebels; *Underline:* claims, **5.** *Circle:* machine; *Draw line through:* among all her appliances; *Underline:* is, **6.** *Circle:* Announcers; *Draw line through:* on this station; *Underline:* seem, **7.** *Circle:* noises; *Draw line through:* from the street; *Underline:* keep, **8.** *Circle:* ramps; *Draw line through:* at the next interchange; *Underline:* are, **9.** *Circle:* score; *Draw line through:* of any student in both classes; *Underline:* is, **10.** *Circle:* mother; *Draw line through:* of twins; *Underline:* needs, **11.** *Circle:* travelers; *Draw line through:* on their way to the historic site; *Underline:* stop

Page 48: 1. *Underline:* daughter, friends; *Circle:* nor; *Underline:* have, **2.** *Underline:* curtains, bedspread; *Circle:* and; *Underline:* need, **3.** *Underline:* rabbits, deer; *Circle:* or; *Underline:* eats, **4.** *Underline:* Antoine, Leo; *Circle:* and; *Underline:* know, **5.** *Underline:* cars, bus; *Circle:* or; *Underline:* fills, **6.** worry, **7.** causes, **8.** hold, **9.** take, **10.** is

Page 49: 1. D, **2.** F, **3.** B, **4.** H, **5.** C, **6.** H, **7.** B, **8.** G

◆ Lesson 9 Adjectives

Page 50: 1. old, apple, pink, 2. bright, green, each, 3. bigger, 4. noisy, new, sports, 5. snowy, largest, 6. most, delicious, 7. long, woolen, warm, 8. last, higher, first

Page 51: 1. (early), earlier, earliest, 2. few, fewer, (fewest), 3. wet, (wetter), wettest, 4. quiet, more quiet, (most quiet), 5. expensive, (less expensive), least expensive, 6. good, (better), best, 7. (large), larger, largest, 8. harder, 9. Correct, 10. worse, 11. Correct

Page 52: 1–8. Answers will vary. Both adjectives for each item must either be in their basic, comparative, or superlative form. 9. fastest, 10. shorter, 11. most delicious, 12. larger, 13. tastier, 14. more beautiful, 15. ripest, 16. brightest

Page 53: 1. A, 2. H, 3. B, 4. F, 5. C, 6. J, 7. D, 8. G

◆ Lesson 10 Adverbs

Page 54: 1. carefully, 2. never, 3. early, 4. busily, 5. rapidly, 6. yesterday, 7. already, 8. faster, 9. slowly, 10. sooner

Page 55: 1–3. (any order) almost, now, well, 4–6. (any order) more rapidly, nearer, more clearly, 7–9. (any order) most gladly, earliest, worst, 10. farthest, 11. better, 12. slowly, 13. Correct, 14. easily, 15. Correct

Page 56: Answers will vary for items 1–5. Possible answers are given for items 6–15. 6. carefully, 7. nervously, 8. more quickly, 9. often, 10. today, 11. earlier, 12. carefully, 13. furiously, 14. today, 15. least frequently

Page 57: 1. C, 2. F, 3. B, 4. J, 5. A, 6. G, 7. D, 8. G

◆ Lesson 11 Adjective or Adverb?

Page 58: 1. adjective, 2. adverb, 3. adverb, 4. adverb, 5. adverb, 6. adjective, 7. adjective, 8. adverb, 9. adjective, 10. adverb

Page 59: 1. brighter, 2. kindly, 3. busiest, 4. nicest, 5. more casually, 6. good, 7. most expensive, 8. more quietly, 9. good, 10. more

interesting, 11. swiftly

Page 60: Answers will vary. Possible answers are provided. 1. careful, 2. easier *or* more attractive, 3. more eagerly, 4. more attractive, 5. deeply, 6. calmer, 7. immediately, 8. happily, 9. youngest *or* calmest *or* happiest, 10. more quickly

Page 61: 1. C, 2. H, 3. A, 4. J, 5. D, 6. H, 7. B, 8. G

◆ Lesson 12 Using Negative Words

Page 62: 1. DN, 2. DN, 3. DN, 4. S, 5. DN, 6. DN, 7. S, 8. DN, 9. S

Page 63: 1. ever, 2. had, 3. any, 4. any, 5. any, 6. anybody, 7. anywhere, 8. could, 9. anything, 10. any, 11. B, 12. A, 13. A, 14. B

Page 64: Answers will vary. Possible answers are provided. 1. Kevin could hardly wait until the weekend. *or* Kevin couldn't wait until the weekend. 2. There isn't anyone who blames you for the accident. *or* No one blames you for the accident. 3. Correct, 4. Can't anybody tell me who won the game? *or* Can nobody tell me who won the game? 5. My dog doesn't ever come when I call. *or* My dog never comes when I call. 6. There was barely enough popcorn for the whole family. *or* There wasn't enough popcorn for the whole family. 7. The pilot hadn't said anything about having a problem. *or* The pilot had said nothing about having a problem. 8. Correct, 9. I never asked for any favors, and I don't expect any. *or* I never asked for favors, and I expect none. 10. I didn't see your cell phone anywhere in the house.

Page 65: 1. B, 2. F, 3. D, 4. H, 5. A, 6. H, 7. B, 8. J

◆ Unit 1 Assessment

Pages 67–69: 1. C, 2. G, 3. A, 4. G, 5. D, 6. H, 7. B, 8. J, 9. B, 10. F, 11. C, 12. H, 13. A, 14. F, 15. B, 16. G, 17. D, 18. G, 19. C, 20. J, 21. H, 22. B, 23. H, 24. D, 25. G, 26. A

◆ Unit 2 Sentence Formation

◆ Lesson 1 Complete Sentences and Fragments

Page 70: 1. F, **2.** CS; *Underline:* Aunt Zelda; *Circle:* loves country music, **3.** CS; *Underline:* cat; *Circle:* broke the lamp, **4.** F, **5.** F, **6.** F, **7.** F, **8.** CS; *Underline:* baby; *Circle:* was hungry, **9.** CS; *Underline:* car; *Circle:* drove up to the house, **10.** F

Page 71: 1. F, **2.** F; Circle sentence and fragment, **3.** CS, **4.** CS, **5.** F, **6.** F; Circle sentence and fragment, **7.** F, **8.** CS, **9.** F; Circle sentence and fragment, **10.** F, **11.** F; Circle both fragments, **12.** CS, **13.** F, **14.** F; Circle sentence and fragment

Page 72: Answers will vary.

Page 73: 1. C, **2.** G, **3.** A, **4.** J, **5.** A, **6.** G

◆ Lesson 2 Run-On Sentences

Page 74: 1. RO, **2.** CS, **3.** RO, **4.** CS, **5.** RO, **6.** CS, **7.** RO, **8.** RO, **9.** RO, **10.** CS

Page 75: 1. RO, **2.** CS, **3.** F, **4.** RO, **5.** RO, **6.** F, **7.** RO, **8.** CS, **9.** RO, **10.** F, **11.** RO, **12.** RO, **13.** CS, **14.** F, **15.** RO, **16.** A, **17.** B, **18.** A

Page 76: Answers will vary. Possible answers are given. **1.** Tara has a new baby. It's a girl. **2.** Spike left town. I haven't seen him in days. **3.** This coffee is weak. I'll make some more. **4.** CS, **5.** I saw the mystic. She said that luck was on its way. **6.** Paul wrote the check. He forgot to sign it. **7.** CS, **8.** John started skateboarding. He's good at it. **9.** CS, **10.** Wiley's is a bookstore. Local authors sometimes speak there.

Page 77: 1. B, **2.** J, **3.** A, **4.** H, **5.** B, **6.** H

◆ Lesson 3 Sentence Combining: Compound Subjects and Predicates

Page 78: 1. The sportswear and shoes must be inventoried. **2.** Correct, **3.** Tulips and daffodils bloom in the spring. **4.** Correct, **5.** My husband and I took dancing lessons. **6.** Diane and Tina interviewed for the job.

Page 79: 1. Alice Jensen gets up early and walks her dog before going to work. **2.** Chris mowed the lawn and pruned the shrubs. **3.** Correct, **4.** The snow covered the ground and drifted against the houses. **5.** Correct, **6.** Erin sat by the window and waited for the rain to stop. **7.** Hailey brushed her hair, braided it carefully, and tied the braids with yellow ribbon.

Page 80: 1. B, **2.** B, **3.** B, **4.** A, **5.** B, **6.** B, **7.** A

Page 81: 1. B, **2.** F, **3.** D, **4.** H

◆ Lesson 4 Sentence Combining: More Compound Sentence Parts

Page 82: 1. *Underline:* The jackhammer is; *Write:* The jackhammer is loud and annoying. **2.** *Underline:* Moyra can speak; *Write:* Moyra can speak Spanish and French. **3.** *Underline:* Ian types/on the computer; *Write:* Ian types letters and reports on the computer. **4.** *Underline:* Mr. Green repairs; *Write:* Mr. Green repairs washing machines and dishwashers. **5.** *Underline:* The diamonds in the necklace are; *Write:* The diamonds in the necklace are beautiful and rare. **6.** *Underline:* The candy machine takes; *Write:* The candy machine takes coins and dollar bills.

Page 83: 1. A, **2.** A, **3.** B, **4.** A, **5.** A, **6.** B

Page 84: 1. Correct, **2.** Remember to pack a raincoat and an umbrella. **3.** Correct, **4.** The bush has broad leaves and red berries. **5.** The customer ordered a cup of coffee and a ham sandwich. **6.** The judges chose Janene quickly and unanimously.

Page 85: 1. C, **2.** G, **3.** A, **4.** G

◆ Lesson 5 Sentence Combining: Adding Modifiers

Page 86: 1. *Underline:* bird; *Write:* A rare bird escaped from the zoo last night. **2.** *Underline:* mountain; *Write:* During their vacation, the Spivaks climbed a mountain in Oregon. **3.** *Underline:* dog; *Write:* A trained dog led her master across the street. **4.** *Underline:* ice-cream; *Write:* This ice-cream in the blue carton tastes like fudge. **5.** *Underline:* sailboat; *Write:* Heath owns a sailboat at Lakeside Dock.

Page 87: 1. Incorrect, **2.** Incorrect, **3.** Correct, **4.** Correct, **5.** Incorrect

Page 88: 1. B, **2.** A, **3.** B, **4.** B, **5.** B, **6.** A

Page 89: 1. D, **2.** G, **3.** A, **4.** H

◆ Lesson 6 Sentence Combining: More About Adding Modifiers

Page 90: 1. C, **2.** A, **3.** E, **4.** B, **5.** D

Page 91: Placement of adverbs and adverb phrases may vary. **1.** The pilot calmly made an emergency announcement. **2.** Two lions silently crept to the water hole. **3.** Flu slowly spread through the office. **4.** Al swam against the current in the river. **5.** Dan and Carole hiked every night for two hours. **6.** Taylor eagerly applied for the job. **7.** We painted the house for three hours before the rain began. **8.** The boat rocked back and forth in the choppy water.

Page 92: Placement of adverbs and adverb phrases may vary. **1.** My son spoke proudly and clearly at his commencement. **2.** Jim entered the county fair through the main gate. **3.** Correct, **4.** The band played "Stars and Stripes Forever" on the Fourth of July. **5.** Correct

Page 93: 1. B, **2.** H, **3.** D, **4.** H

◆ Unit 2 Assessment

Pages 95–97: 1. D, **2.** F, **3.** C, **4.** G, **5.** B, **6.** F, **7.** D, **8.** F, **9.** B, **10.** B, **11.** F, **12.** D, **13.** H

◆ Unit 3 Paragraph Development

◆ Lesson 1 The Topic Sentence of a Paragraph

Page 98: 1. B, **2.** G

Page 99: 1. D, **2.** A, **3.** B, **4.** E, **5.** C

Page 100: Answers will vary. Possible answers are given. **1.** Elvis was a musical superstar. **2.** Jaguars and pumas are alike in many ways. **3.** There are many kinds of tomatoes. **4.** You can have eggs a different way every day.

Page 101: 1. B, **2.** F, **3.** A, **4.** G

◆ Lesson 2 Finding the Topic Sentence

Page 102: 1. *Underline:* There are two main kinds of coffee: arabica and robusta. **2.** *Underline:* Mexico is a land of diverse climates. **3.** *Underline:* Windsurfing has become a popular sport all over the world.

Page 103: 1. B, **2.** F, **3.** D

Page 104: Answers will vary. Possible answers are given. **1.** Bears eat large quantities of food. **2.** Different kinds of fireworks produce different effects. **3.** Elephants communicate using sound. **4.** There are many kinds of dental specialists.

Page 105: 1. A, **2.** J, **3.** C

◆ Lesson 3 Developing Paragraphs with Details and Examples

Page 106: 1. supporting sentence, **2.** topic sentence

Page 107: 1. examples, **2.** sensory details, **3.** examples, **4.** examples, **5.** sensory details

Page 108: Answers will vary.

Page 109: 1. D, **2.** H, **3.** B

◆ Lesson 4 Developing Paragraphs with Facts, Figures, and Reasons

Page 110: 1. topic sentence, **2.** supporting sentence

Page 111: 1. facts and figures, **2.** reasons, **3.** facts and figures, **4.** reasons, **5.** facts and figures

Page 112: Answers will vary.

Page 113: 1. B, **2.** J, **3.** C

◆ Lesson 5 Recognizing Sequence Using Key Words

Page 114: **1.** C, **2.** G

Page 115: Answers will vary. Possible answers are given. **1.** The raven dropped pebbles to make islands. **2.** The raven created trees and grass. **3.** The raven made beasts. **4.** The raven made birds and fish. **5.** The raven made man and woman. **6.** The students held a bake sale and a car wash. **7.** They bought old furniture. **8.** They refinished the furniture. **9.** They sold the furniture. **10.** They sent the money to the relief fund.

Page 116: **1.** first, third, second, finally, **2.** first, finally, third, second, **3.** third, first, finally, second, **4.** third, finally, first, second

Page 117: **1.** D, **2.** G, **3.** D

◆ Lesson 6 Recognizing Sequence Without Using Key Words

Page 118: **1.** C, **2.** H

Page 119: **1.** D, **2.** B, **3.** A, **4.** C

Page 120: **1.** 4, 3, 1, 2, **2.** 3, 1, 2, 4, **3.** 1, 4, 2, 3, **4.** 3, 4, 2, 1

Page 121: **1.** D, **2.** G, **3.** A

◆ Lesson 7 Identifying the Unrelated Sentence

Page 122: **1.** B, **2.** H

Page 123: Wording of answers will vary. Possible answers: **1.** *Cross out:* Stewart was born in 1908. *Reason:* It does not tell more about why Stewart was popular. **2.** *Cross out:* Lifeguards must pass difficult tests. *Reason:* It does not tell how the pool affected Lynn's summer. **3.** *Cross out:* His brother has a job at the garage. *Reason:* It does not relate to Joe's efforts to find a job. **4.** *Cross out:* Flowers need plenty of water and sunlight. *Reason:* It does not describe a way in which the garden was beautiful.

Page 124: **1.** *Cross out:* I am glad that I don't have to clean those floors. **2.** *Cross out:* Soil is made up of tiny bits of rock. **3.** *Cross out:* Basements can be damp and chilly. **4.** Correct, **5.** *Cross out:* Swing was popular in the 1940s.

Page 125: **1.** B, **2.** J, **3.** C, **4.** H

◆ Unit 3 Assessment

Pages 127–129: **1.** C, **2.** F, **3.** B, **4.** J, **5.** H, **6.** B, **7.** J, **8.** D, **9.** H, **10.** D, **11.** G

◆ Unit 4 Capitalization

◆ Lesson 1 Capitalizing Proper Nouns

Page 130: **1.** Mrs. Helen Jacobs, **2.** E. H. Yates, **3.** Uncle Milton, **4.** Mr., Mrs. Fulton, **5.** Aunt Sonya, Dr. Harris, **6.** Mayor Henson, **7.** John Philip Sousa, **8.** Ms. Moore, **9.** Joyce, Leann, Stacy, **10.** Coach Rodriguez

Page 131: **1.** Mrs. Karen Robinson, **2.** Correct, **3.** Senator Barbara Glenn, **4.** Jackson A. Perkins, **5.** Aunt Diana, **6.** Queen Elizabeth, **7.** Captain Paul D. Daniels, **8.** Correct, **9.** Dr. Carl Williams, **10.** Carla M. Ramirez, **11.** B, **12.** B, **13.** A, **14.** B

Page 132: **1.** Are you here to see Mr. L. B. Taylor *or* Mr. J. F. Taylor? **2.** This story was written by A. A. Milne. **3.** Last week I had dinner with Aunt Josie and Uncle George. **4.** Will Dr. Lee please come to the front desk? **5.** Give the letter to Ms. Sara Brenner. **6.** There is a picture of Governor Keller in the newspaper. **7.** Did Aunt Doris get the tools that belonged to our grandfather? **8.** This is the office of Judge Kathleen Marshall. **9.** I enjoyed the book by Robert L. Stevenson. **10.** She, Marcella, and Kim share an office.

Page 133: **1.** B, **2.** H, **3.** A, **4.** H, **5.** B, **6.** J, **7.** C, **8.** G

◆ Lesson 2 Capitalizing Proper Nouns and Proper Adjectives

Page 134: **1.** Halloween, Friday, October, **2.** Granada High School, Wall Street, **3.** Eiffel Tower, Paris, France, **4.** Ohio River,

5. French, 6. Painted Desert, Arizona,
7. Huron Avenue, 8. Russian, New York,
9. Labor Day, September, American,
10. Niagara Falls, Niagara River

Page 135: 1. Monday, 2. Correct, 3. Canada,
4. Rodeo Drive, 5. Atlantic Ocean, 6. Swiss,
7. Nebraska, 8. Correct, 9. B, 10. B, 11. B,
12. A, 13. A, 14. B

Page 136: 1. I start my new job on Tuesday,
June 4. 2. We can meet at the corner of
Collins Drive and Concord Road. 3. Were
the Chinese people the first to make paper?
4. The sport of surfing began in Hawaii.
5. Be sure to visit the Statue of Liberty
when you are in New York City. 6. The city
of Chicago, Illinois, is next to Lake
Michigan. 7. We celebrate Thanksgiving in
November. 8. The Thames River flows
through London, England. 9. I have to work
one Saturday every month. 10. Many
people in Mexico speak both the Spanish
and the English language.

Page 137: 1. B, 2. H, 3. A, 4. J, 5. C, 6. G

◆ Lesson 3 Capitalizing First Words and Titles

Page 138: 1. Remember, 2. The, What,
3. My, *Howl's Moving Castle*, 4. Where,
5. Most, The Three Billy Goats Gruff, 6. The,
Move, 7. The, *The Phantom, Opera*, 8. How,
9. One, *Beauty, Beast*, 10. Building, Deck,
Your, Garden, Home

Page 139: 1. *The Last of the Mohicans*, 2. "By
the Waters of Babylon", 3. "The Raven",
4. Correct, 5. "All in the Family", 6. *House
and Garden*, 7. Correct, 8. *The Catcher in the
Rye*, 9. B, 10. B, 11. B, 12. A, 13. A, 14. A

Page 140: 1. Did you watch "Law and
Order" last night? 2. We enjoy the stories in
the Reader's Digest. 3. The umpire yelled,
"Strike three!" 4. Many people think Citizen
Kane is a great movie. 5. The zoo keeper
told us, "The lion cub is only one month
old." 6. "Brush your teeth twice a day," said
the dentist. 7. We read the poem "Stopping
by Woods on a Snowy Evening." 8. "How
much does this shirt cost?" asked the
customer. 9. My boss said, "Mail these

letters." 10. "This bus is always late,"
complained the passengers.

Page 141: 1. B, 2. H, 3. A, 4. J, 5. D, 6. F, 7. C,
8. G

◆ Unit 4 Assessment

Pages 143–145: 1. B, 2. H, 3. A, 4. G, 5. B,
6. J, 7. B, 8. J, 9. G, 10. C, 11. F, 12. A, 13. F,
14. H, 15. A, 16. J, 17. D, 18. F, 19. B, 20. F,
21. C

◆ Unit 5 Punctuation

◆ Lesson 1 End Marks

Page 146: 1. ? 2. . 3. ! 4. ! *or* . 5. . 6. . 7. ? 8. !
9. . 10. !

Page 147: 1. A, 2. G, 3. C, 4. H, 5. B, 6. F,
7. A, 8. A, 9. B, 10. B, 11. B, 12. B

Page 148: Sentences will vary. They should
all relate to the given situations and end
with the proper end marks.

Page 149: 1. B, 2. F, 3. D, 4. H, 5. B, 6. J, 7. B,
8. H, 9. B, 10. F, 11. C, 12. G

◆ Lesson 2 Commas in Compound Sentences

Page 150: 1. B, 2. A, 3. A, 4. A, 5. B, 6. B

Page 151: 1. B, 2. F, 3. B, 4. H, 5. A,
6. Correct, 7. insert comma after *closed*,
8. insert comma after *myself*, 9. insert comma
after *work*, 10. Correct, 11. insert comma
after *pizza*, 12. insert comma after *roads*

Page 152: 1. Correct, 2. *X* on comma,
3. insert comma after *early*, 4. insert comma
after *gloomy*, 5. *X* on comma, 6. insert
comma after *night*, 7. *X* on comma,
8. Correct, 9. Correct, 10. *X* on comma, 11. *X*
on comma, 12. insert comma after *empty*,
13. Correct, 14. insert comma after *foods*,
15. insert comma after *night*

Page 153: 1. C, 2. F, 3. D, 4. H, 5. A, 6. G,
7. B, 8. H

◆ Lesson 3 Commas in Series

Page 154: 1. insert commas after *dogs, cats*,
2. insert commas after *plums, peaches*,

3. insert commas after *exercised, weights,*
4. Correct, **5.** insert commas after *Tim, Tom, Ray,* **6.** Correct, **7.** insert commas after *sodas, milkshakes,* **8.** insert commas after *twirls, jumps,* **9.** insert commas after *Tan, Chung,* **10.** insert commas after *lions, tigers*

Page 155: **1.** A, **2.** B, **3.** B, **4.** A, **5.** A, **6.** insert commas after *papers, mail,* **7.** Correct, **8.** insert commas after *red, yellow,* **9.** insert commas after *beef, chicken,* **10.** insert commas after *Robins, crows, doves,* **11.** insert commas after *tent, bag*

Page 156: **1.** insert commas after *shed, porch,* **2.** insert commas after *Ali, Ivan, Chu,* **3.** insert commas after *still, camera,* **4.** insert commas after *Books, papers,* **5.** insert commas after *sand, clay,* **6.** insert commas after *bank, shop,* **7.** insert commas after *gum, candy,* **8.** insert commas after *chocolate, vanilla,* **9.** insert commas after *buns, bread,* **10.** insert commas after *cheered, waved,* **11.** insert commas after *Oz, Poppins,* **12.** insert commas after *terrier, shepherd,* **13.** insert commas after *mother, father,* **14.** Correct, **15.** insert commas after *woods, lake,* **16.** insert commas after *car, van*

Page 157: **1.** B, **2.** H, **3.** A, **4.** G, **5.** D, **6.** F, **7.** C, **8.** J

◆ Lesson 4 Other Uses of Commas

Page 158: **1.** B, **2.** A, **3.** A, **4.** A, **5.** B, **6.** A, **7.** A

Page 159: **1.** Dale, **2.** Paula, **3.** Ladies and gentlemen, **4.** Jen, **5.** Brother, **6.** You silly dog, **7.** insert comma after *stick,* **8.** insert comma after *spell,* **9.** insert comma after *seats,* **10.** insert comma after *Rachel,* **11.** insert comma after *country,* **12.** insert comma after *Yes,* **13.** insert comma after *today,* **14.** insert comma after *weather,* **15.** insert commas after *book, sir*

Page 160: **1.** insert comma after *broken,* **2.** insert commas after *Yes, today,* **3.** insert comma after *dinner,* **4.** insert commas after *think, Dan,* **5.** insert comma after *lemonade,* **6.** insert comma after *backpack,* **7.** insert commas after *raining, porch,* **8.** no comma

needed, **9.** insert commas after *snacks, Seth,* **10.** insert commas after *No, dear*

Page 161: **1.** C, **2.** G, **3.** D, **4.** F, **5.** B, **6.** J, **7.** C, **8.** G

◆ Unit 5 Assessment

Pages 163–165: **1.** C, **2.** J, **3.** A, **4.** F, **5.** B, **6.** H, **7.** C, **8.** F, **9.** A, **10.** G, **11.** C, **12.** G, **13.** A, **14.** G, **15.** C, **16.** J, **17.** B, **18.** H, **19.** D, **20.** F, **21.** B, **22.** G, **23.** A

◆ Unit 6 Writing Conventions

◆ Lesson 1 Direct and Indirect Quotations

Page 166: **1.** The coach shouted, "Line up along the fence!" **2.** Indirect, **3.** "Will this be on your credit card?" asked the clerk. **4.** Patrick Henry bravely said, "Give me liberty, or give me death." **5.** "Who just rang the bell?" asked Naomi. **6.** Indirect, **7.** Indirect, **8.** After she fell, the toddler cried, "I want my mama!" **9.** Indirect

Page 167: Sentences may vary slightly. Possible answers are given. **1.** Kyle asked what the score was. **2.** The pilot announced that we will land in about twenty minutes. **3.** Nicole complained that her sunburn really hurt. **4.** The ranger said, "Boil your water before drinking it." **5.** The weather forecaster said, "Today will be sunny." **6.** The guard at the door asked, "Are you members?" **7.** A, **8.** A, **9.** B, **10.** A

Page 168: **1.** The nurse said, "The doctor will see you now." **2.** Indirect, **3.** Joshua suggested, "Let's get a cup of coffee and a piece of pie." **4.** "The fire is out of control!" shouted the cook. **5.** The detective asked, "When did you discover the jewels were missing?" **6.** Indirect, **7.** "Would you like to rent a video?" asked Steve. **8.** Katy pleaded, "Give me just one taste of your banana split!" **9.** Indirect, **10.** Indirect

Page 169: **1.** C, **2.** F, **3.** B, **4.** H, **5.** A, **6.** J, **7.** B, **8.** H

◆ Lesson 2 Using Commas with Quotations

Page 170: 1. The repairman said, "This will cost about fifty dollars." **2.** "Put your bags in the overhead bin," said the attendant. **3.** "I saw a good movie last night," reported Mia. **4.** Hector shouted, "Slide!" **5.** "My car is making a funny noise," said Grace. **6.** Kristen complained, "That was a really bad pun!" **7.** The rules clearly state, "The game ends when one player earns 100 points." **8.** "Roses need plenty of sunlight and water," said Mrs. White. **9.** Paul moaned, "My house needs painting again!" **10.** Justin said, "Let's find a seat near the stage." **11.** "We will be there in time for the next movie," said Julio.

Page 171: 1. "That movie got good reviews," Lucia said. **2.** "The brakes on my car failed," the driver explained. **3.** "Your total is ten dollars," the clerk said. **4.** Andy said, "Save me a seat." **5.** Alicia whispered, "The baby just went to sleep." **6.** Heather's aunt said, "Always wear sunscreen." **7.** B, **8.** A

Page 172: 1. "I hope I get this job," said Julie. **2.** Sonya asked, "Will you need a packed lunch today?" **3.** Correct, **4.** The governor announced, "The budget is in good shape." **5.** "My house has been for sale for six months," Bill told his friend. **6.** Correct, **7.** "Watch what I do," said the dance teacher. **8.** Luis said, "I'm looking for a good used car." **9.** "I'll answer the phone during lunch hour," Gina told her coworkers. **10.** Correct

Page 173: 1. C, **2.** G, **3.** D, **4.** F, **5.** A, **6.** J, **7.** B, **8.** H

◆ Lesson 3 Contractions

Page 174: 1. did + not, **2.** he + is, **3.** should + not, **4.** we + will, **5.** I + am, **6.** they + are, **7.** you + will, **8.** she + will, **9.** was + not, **10.** will + not, **11.** can't, **12.** haven't, **13.** weren't, **14.** isn't, **15.** won't, **16.** we're

Page 175: 1. A, **2.** B, **3.** A, **4.** B, **5.** Laura couldn't recall the important phone number. **6.** We'll take a break at 10 A.M. **7.** We're glad that you came. **8.** It's not like him to be so late. **9.** I'd like to join you, but I can't. **10.** I'm sure that you'll be pleased with the results.

Page 176: Sentences will vary. All answers must include at least one correctly written contraction.

Page 177: 1. A, **2.** G, **3.** C, **4.** J, **5.** B, **6.** F, **7.** D, **8.** H

◆ Lesson 4 Possessive Nouns

Page 178: 1. Laura's, S, **2.** Isaiah's, S, **3.** squirrels', P, **4.** flowers', P, **5.** artist's, S, **6.** captain's, S, **7.** sisters', P, **8.** driver's, S, **9.** women's, P, **10.** doctors', P

Page 179: 1. B, **2.** B, **3.** A, **4.** B, **5.** A, **6.** that nurse's station, **7.** the tellers' windows, **8.** the plumber's tools, **9.** the voters' rights, **10.** the robbers' footprints, **11.** the men's league, **12.** the children's games, **13.** the princess's fortune, **14.** the king's orders

Page 180: 1. builder's, **2.** Correct, **3.** sorcerer's, **4.** patients', **5.** waitress's, **6.** children's, **7.** Correct, **8.** foreman's, **9.** Bakers', **10.** man's, **11.** bears'

Page 181: 1. B, **2.** H, **3.** A, **4.** J, **5.** B, **6.** G, **7.** A, **8.** H

◆ Lesson 5 Letter Parts

Page 182: 1. 386 March Avenue **2.** Sincerely yours, **3.** Dear Sir or Madam: **4.** April 8, 2004

Page 183: *Heading*: September 6, 2003 *Inside Address*: (line 1) What-a-Buy Appliances (line 2) 213 Oak Street (line 3) Livermore, California 94550 *Greeting*: Dear Sir or Madam: *Body*: I am writing in response to your ad for a sales clerk in your store. I am very familiar with the video and audio equipment you sell. Please send me an application for the job. *Closing*: Respectfully yours, *Signature and Name*: *Tiera King* Tiera King

Page 184: The wording of the body of the letter may vary. The heading, inside address, greeting, and closing must be capitalized and punctuated correctly.

Page 185: 1. B, 2. H, 3. D, 4. F, 5. B

◆ Unit 6 Assessment

Pages 187–189: 1. B, 2. H, 3. C, 4. F, 5. D,
6. G, 7. A, 8. J, 9. A, 10. H, 11. B, 12. F, 13. C,
14. G, 15. D, 16. H, 17. B, 18. F, 19. A, 20. H